GW00802205

TEACHING THE HANDICAPPED CHILD

TEACHING
THE HANDICAPPED
CHILD

by

Dorothy M. Jeffree, Roy McConkey, Simon Hewson

A CONDOR BOOK
SOUVENIR PRESS (E & A) LTD

First published 1977 by Souvenir Press (Educational & Academic) Ltd,
43 Great Russell Street, London WC1B 3PA
and simultaneously in Canada

Reprinted 1979

ISBN 0 285 64838 1 casebound
ISBN 0 285 64839 x paperback

Printed in Great Britain by
Clarke, Doble & Brendon Ltd,
Plymouth and London

ACKNOWLEDGEMENTS

Much of the content of this book derives from our work on the Parental Involvement Project. The project was financed jointly by the Department of Health and Social Security and the Department of Education and Science, and was based at the Hester Adrian Research Centre, University of Manchester.

During the project we worked closely with many handicapped children and their families. We also came in contact with many interested parents and professionals from all over the country. Their eagerness to help handicapped children was a great source of encouragement and inspiration to us. We would like to thank them for that.

Our thanks also to Betty Carrington for typing the manuscript.

Contents

A *

Preface

This book is primarily designed as a companion volume to our
'Let Me . . .' books.

In books such as *Let Me Speak*, our emphasis has been on
specific teaching games to help handicapped children learn new
skills. But this book is different. Our emphasis here is on an
overall approach to teaching, irrespective of its specific content.
In this book we try to provide some guidelines to help parents
and professionals find answers to the four questions they most
frequently ask when it comes to teaching a handicapped child:
questions such as—

What can I expect the child to learn? In Section 1, we examine
teaching objectives and how teachers can set about choosing
them.

How can I help the child to learn? In Section 2, we describe
teaching approaches and techniques which are common to all
learning situations.

Are we doing all right? In Section 3, we outline ways of assessing
progress. This involves examining the teacher as well as the
child.

Whom can I get to help? In Section 4, we suggest ways of involving
others in the teaching, and concentrate particularly on home-
school links and inter-professional contact.

Throughout the book we intend the word 'teacher' to be
taken in its widest sense, i.e. any person who is trying to help
the child to learn is a teacher. This of course includes parents
as well as professionals, such as teachers in school, psychologists
and therapists. We hope that all these teachers will find the

book useful. However, we do have to admit that when writing the book we often had the professional teacher in mind. So in many ways, the book is primarily for them. However, this book is by no means a comprehensive text on the education of handicapped children. We realise that there are many other aspects to education and child development which we have not touched upon. Rather our aim here is to describe a teaching approach that we and others have found to be useful. We believe it will prove helpful to other teachers of handicapped children.

Introduction

No two children are alike; they vary in their abilities, temperament, interests and needs. Handicapped children are just as individual. Indeed we cannot talk of a typical handicapped child. Different handicaps can have very different effects. For example, the effects of blindness are not the same as those of deafness. The severity of the handicap can also vary. A child's hearing may be partially lost or he may be almost totally deaf. Also, a child may have one predominant handicap, or he may be multiply handicapped.

Thus the type, severity and number of handicapping disorders add to the diversity among handicapped children.

Yet these children do all have one thing in common. Their handicap invariably interferes with their learning. We take the view that learning primarily occurs as a result of the child's interaction with his environment, i.e. the people, objects and events in the world around him. Anything that interferes with that interaction, e.g. a handicap such as deafness, will mean that learning is made more difficult; with the consequence that the child's development is delayed. But the amount and type of delay will vary from child to child. For each individual child there will be a pattern of strengths and weaknesses, thus for instance a child's physical development may be greatly delayed, but his language development may be relatively unaffected. This unevenness in development is one of the hallmarks of handicapped children.

However, we do know that with help, the effects of handicaps on learning can often be reduced and even removed. This help can take many different forms, but perhaps most important is the help the child receives from his teachers. Now a teacher can be anyone who wants to help a child to learn. Thus parents, brothers and sisters, even neighbours, can all be called teachers, as well as the professional teachers or therapists.

If the teacher's help is to be really effective, then it must be carefully matched to the child's present abilities. All new learning is dependent on past learning. So the teacher must make a careful appraisal of each child's particular abilities, needs and interests, if she is to be successful at helping his learning. Indeed, it is for this reason that we called this book 'Teaching *the* Handicapped Child'. But we must stress that there are no teaching methods that will invariably help the child to learn. There is no 'cook-book' that the teacher can use and there never will be. Helping an individual child to learn is, in one sense, an experiment. The outcome cannot always be predicted, but we can still obtain valuable information, even if the results are unexpected and perhaps disappointing. Thus the teacher cannot take anything for granted. She must check that her teaching really is helping the child's learning.

The teacher of a handicapped child faces many challenges. To be successful she has to be even more systematic and thoughtful in her approach than, say, the teacher of normal children. This is the main theme of this book, and our aim in writing it is to help teachers, whether parents or professionals, to develop such an approach.

Three stages of teaching
This systematic approach can be conceived of as a three-stage cycle.

Stage 1: Choosing teaching objectives. The starting point is a detailed appraisal of what the child can do. This will enable the teacher to select specific objectives. It will then be easier to plan teaching schemes and to monitor the child's progress. We examine this stage in Section 1 (page 21).

Stage 2: Helping the child to learn. Having selected her objectives, the teacher has to consider how best to help the child to learn. She can become much more effective at doing this by choosing favourable conditions for learning and by consistently applying specific teaching techniques. In Section 2 (page 57) we will discuss these topics.

Stage 3: Assessing progress. Finally, it is most important to monitor the child's progress. For if there is no sign of progress we will have to re-appraise our choice of teaching methods and teaching objectives. Conversely, if the objective is attained we can then move on. This third stage is crucial, for with it the cycle is complete. We deal with this stage in Section 3 (page 115).

Assumptions underlying our approach

We feel we should make clear at the outset some of the influences and assumptions which are central in our approach to teaching the handicapped child.

1. Development of basic skills

We are primarily concerned with the development of basic skills, such as reaching and grasping, walking, imitation, using language. Our reason for calling such skills *basic*, is that often they are involved in so many of the child's activities and are used in lots of situations. But perhaps most importantly, these skills are an essential foundation to the child's future learning. Once he has acquired these skills, he can begin to move 'under his own steam', and is less dependent on others.

There are other aspects of a child's development with which we shall not deal directly, e.g. emotional or personality development. This is not to imply that we feel these are unimportant. Rather we focus on the acquisition of basic skills because these seem to underlie many diverse aspects of a child's development.

2. Normal child development

We have been much influenced by the idea emerging from studies of normal child development, that underpinning the development of basic skills there is a hierarchy of pre-requisite skills. For example, some of the skills a child requires before he can even name a single object are articulation, comprehension and imitation. Often our teaching has to be aimed in the first instance at helping the child to acquire these pre-requisite skills.

3. Play

Children often develop and practice these pre-requisite skills through play. Thus, within the systematic teaching approach, we place great store on the need for teachers to encourage children's play. However, with handicapped children, teachers will often need to help the children by structuring their play, e.g. in the teaching games described in the 'Let Me' books. Yet it is equally important that we give them plenty of opportunities for initiating and directing their own play.

Practical points

On the practical side, we feel that the following points are important to successful teaching:

1. Regular teaching sessions

We feel that handicapped children benefit particularly from regular sessions with a teacher. This repetition, centred around specific topics, helps children to work out what they are expected to learn and gives them the opportunity to practice their new skills.

2. One-to-One teaching

We stressed earlier how varied handicapped children are in their abilities, interests, and so on. To be successful, the teaching has to be closely matched to the child's present abilities. This requires the teacher to plan her teaching very much on an individual basis, and often to carry it out in a one-to-one setting. However, this need not necessarily be in a separate room or even for long periods of time; much can be done in two or three minutes. Indeed, there are many occasions in the course of a day when even busy teachers deal with only one child at a time. Short but regular sessions have much to commend them.

3. Working together

Helping a child to learn can normally never be the sole prerogative of one person. As we noted earlier, a child can have many teachers. With the handicapped child it is vitally important that his teachers work together, for only then will the child receive the optimal help. It is for this reason that we place great stress upon a teaching partnership between parents and professionals, and close inter-professional contact. Indeed, we have devoted Section 4 of the book to this theme of working together (see page 175).

CHOOSING AMONG ALTERNATIVES

One thing which we should make clear is that this systematic approach to teaching is very demanding on the teacher. This may not be in terms of work-load or energy expended, although it may well be; but it is very demanding in terms of *thinking*. Successful teaching requires careful planning. And the most important aspect of this planning is the teacher's choice among the many alternatives open to her at any given time. For as soon as a teacher decides that she is going to help a child to learn, she is immediately confronted with such choices as 'which objective is appropriate for the child?', or 'which teaching game shall I use?'. And the difficulty all teachers face is that there are no hard and fast rules which they can follow. Each decision has to be thought out anew.

Throughout this book, and especially in the 'Let Me' books, we do try to give teachers some guidelines to follow in choosing teaching objectives or teaching games. However, the right decisions will be made only if based on sound information. Knowing about the child's abilities and interests is an important part of that information, but in itself is insufficient. You also need to know—

(a) how children learn, or more correctly, how *we* think they learn, i.e. theories of child development;

(b) where all your teaching is leading, i.e. your own educational philosophy.

Theories of child development

Although we can easily observe the different stages children go through in learning new skills (c.f. Developmental Charts, see page 23), we can only speculate as to how the learning takes place. Nevertheless, if we as teachers are to help handicapped children develop new skills, we need to have some idea as to *how* children normally acquire them. In particular, the theories of child development can inform the teacher as to (i) pre-requisite skills, and (ii) 'appropriate' conditions for learning. Theories can be crudely classed into two kinds: (a) overall theories of development, e.g. Piaget, Bruner; and (b) theories related to specific aspects of development, e.g. Bloom's theory of early language acquisition. Obviously, it would be impossible for us even to begin to summarise any of these theories. Suffice it to say that we have often had them in mind when planning teaching schemes for individual children, and that many of the guidelines given to teachers in books such as *Let Me Speak* derive from particular theories of development.

We would urge teachers to become familiar with some of the more influential theories. There is no one adequate or totally accepted theory of child development, so in reading about different theories, treat them as sources of ideas which you should put to the 'test' in your teaching.

Educational philosophy

It is not enough just to know which skills you want the child to learn. You also need to know *why* he should learn them. The answer you give to the question 'why' is a reflection of your aims for the child and of your educational philosophy. There are no absolute answers, for now you are in the realm of ideals, attitudes, beliefs and even politics. And nobody can give you a definitive answer; you have to make up your own mind.

Society's attitude to the handicapped has undergone a number of changes during this century, especially as regards their integration into the community. Similarly, our philosophy of education for the handicapped is still evolving. We who are presently teaching handicapped children are instrumental in shaping that philosophy. All the more reason for each of us to give careful thought to the question of why we have chosen to teach the child a specific skill.

But your educational philosophy should enter into all aspects of your teaching; for example, in your choice of teaching methods. Suppose that you want the child to be able to find toilets, particular bus-stops, etc. Do you spend your time teaching him a social-sight vocabulary so that he will recognise the appropriate signs, or do you encourage him instead to ask other people for the information? You could reach your objective by either method, but we would argue that your choice of method is a reflection of your philosophy.

Equally, having a clear idea of your aims for a child enables you to assess your priorities. Often handicapped children require help in many different ways, but which needs are the most urgent? If our time and resources are limited, then we have to work on the basis of priorities. For example, in helping the child to learn to use words, do you concentrate on words like 'Ta' or 'Please' that will make him socially acceptable, or do you give priority to words that will convey a message like 'tea' or 'give me'? Do you let him take part in physical activities such as climbing stairs, even though there is a risk he will hurt himself? Is your priority to encourage exploration or to protect him?

As teachers we will continually be faced with questions like these. Knowing where you are going, and why, is the only way of resolving them. Furthermore, you continually need to check that your short-term objectives are leading in the direction you want to go. You must not lose sight of your aims. Otherwise you will merely be teaching the child certain skills which at best are 'task-specific', and at worse merely 'tricks'.

Thus the systematic approach which we will concentrate on

in this book should cause the teacher to think carefully about what she is doing. But the only way you will develop a thoughtful approach is through the experience of trying it out. Simply reading this book will not make you a better teacher; you will become more effective only through putting the ideas into practice.

SECTION 1: CHOOSING TEACHING OBJECTIVES

Introduction

One of the first questions that you, as a teacher of a handicapped child, will ask yourself is, 'What am I going to teach him?' Our purpose, in the next three chapters, is to show you how you can answer this question.

In the Introduction to the book we made the point that all new learning depends in part on what the learner is already capable of, on what he has already learned. We also stressed that handicapped children are highly individual people, meaning that each child will show a unique blend of abilities, needs and interests. The significance of these points for the teacher is that unless she knows what are the individual child's abilities, needs and interests, she will not really be in a position to help that child's development.

So the first step in teaching a handicapped child is, paradoxically, to stop being a teacher. Instead, you must become a learner. You have to get to know the child whom you intend to teach.

This point may seem obvious, but is it really? Teachers are typically cast in the role of 'those who know', and to be found not to know is often considered a failing, even a disgrace. We expect our doctor to know what to prescribe when we are ill, and we expect our garage mechanic to know how to fix the car when it breaks down. Similarly, it is presumed that a teacher should know what to teach any particular child.

We believe that this attitude is both unfair and dangerous. It is unfair because, as we have already stressed, handicapped children are so individual that no teacher can be expected to know automatically what to teach each one. Secondly, it is dangerous because it may prevent a teacher from finding out what she is already expected to know. It can be very difficult, when confronted by someone who thinks that you have, or should have, all the answers, to say, 'I honestly don't know'.

Yet this is the necessary starting point when you begin to teach a handicapped child, to say 'I don't know, but I'm going to find out'.

In order to find out what to teach a child, you will first have to get to know very thoroughly what the child can and cannot do. In the next two chapters we want to suggest some ways in which you can acquire this knowledge.

In Chapter 1, **An Initial Assessment**, we consider how you can build up an initial profile of the child's level of development, by finding out his overall strengths and weaknesses. This initial profile is very useful in guiding you towards particular areas of development in which the child needs the most help.

However, in order to design teaching schemes to suit the individual child, you will often require more specific information. Therefore, in Chapter 2, **Looking Closer**, we consider how you can make more detailed observations of the child and how this information will help you to plan your teaching schemes.

But in order to devise appropriate teaching schemes, you must also know precisely what you want the child to learn. Therefore, in Chapter 3, **The Teaching Objective**, we consider the importance of clearly stated teaching objectives and how they can benefit your teaching activities.

1 : An Initial Assessment

The purpose of an initial assessment of the child is to build up an overall picture of the child's developmental strengths and weaknesses. Assessment, therefore, involves observing the child in a variety of activities in order to find out what he can and cannot do. However, observation does not mean simply looking at the child. We also have to know what we are looking for. In other words, we need a frame of reference which will guide our observations.

In our initial assessment of the child we use as our guide the PIP Developmental Charts. These charts, which are devised specifically for the purposes of assessment, are published in Britain by Hodder and Stoughton (Educational), P.O. Box 702, Mill Road, Dunton Green, Sevenoaks, Kent TW13 2YD. Sections of the charts are also reproduced in two of our books; *Let Me Speak* and *Let Me Play*.

Of course, these are not the only development charts in existence. Individual charts vary in the types of development which they cover and none should be considered exhaustive. For example, the PIP Developmental Charts do not deal directly with emotional development and personality development. But they do reflect our chief interests in this book, namely, the development of those basic skills which the child needs in order to understand and to adapt to the world in which he is growing up.

Your choice of particular charts will no doubt be governed by their availability and your preferences. However, we would like to explain how the charts can be used for assessing the child, and we shall do this with references to our own PIP Developmental Charts.

The PIP Developmental Charts
The charts outline the development of skills which children

usually acquire during the first five years of life. The skills are grouped into five major areas:

(1) Physical Development.
(2) Social Development.
(3) Eye-Hand Development.
(4) Development of Play.
(5) Language Development.

Each major skill area is further divided into sections. For example, Eye-Hand Development is divided into three sections:

(a) Reaching.
(b) Grasping.
(c) Objects.

It would be preferable if you read this chapter in conjunction with a copy of the Developmental Charts. For convenience, we have reproduced in Figure 1 the section on Objects.

SECTION II: OBJECTS

(18)	Searches actively and appropriately for a toy—looks in cupboards, etc.	YES	NO
(15)	Looks in correct place for toys that have rolled out of sight	YES	NO
(11)	Finds a toy if he sees it hidden in a box	YES	NO
(10)	Chooses a toy if he has seen it hidden by a cloth	YES	NO
(9)	Looks for dropped toys	YES	NO
(6)	Will look for toys if they roll just out of reach	YES	NO
(3)	If given a toy will show some interest in it	YES	NO

Figure 1. An Example taken from the PIP. Developmental
Charts

This chart describes the developmental stages through which a young child progresses as he gradually builds up his understanding about objects in the world around him. The figures in brackets give the age, in months, at which children normally reach each particular level of development. However, bear in mind that these ages are only approximate and could be found to vary quite considerably even among normal children. What is much more important in assessing a handicapped child is to know about the ordered sequence of developmental stages in each skill area, and to be able to find the child's level of development of each particular skill.

The 'Objects' chart is only one section of the charts dealing with the child's Eye-Hand Development, which in turn is only one of the five main areas of development represented in the Developmental Charts. This will give you some idea of just how comprehensively you can assess the child through the Developmental Charts.

How do we use the charts? As Figure 1 illustrates, the charts may be used very simply in 'checklist' fashion. You tick the 'YES' box for those items which the child can do and you tick the 'NO' box for those items which the child has not yet achieved. (The Developmental Charts provide more detailed instructions for working through them.) In this way, you can gauge the child's level of development in each skill area.

Direct observation. All the items in the Charts describe an observable activity. This means that you need be in no doubt as to whether the child is capable of a particular item. If you are at all unsure of the child's abilities, do not rely on hazy recollections, or, worse still, the hearsay of others. Find out for yourself by observing the child specifically on that item.

Queries? You may find, of course, that having observed the child, you are still unsure whether the answer is 'YES' or 'NO'. This may be because the answer is both 'YES' and 'NO'—the child only shows the behaviour some of the time. This may be because the child was either tired or uninterested at the time he was observed. In this case, defer your decision until you have assessed him under more favourable conditions.

However, it is also possible that the child's intermittent behaviour indicates that he has not fully mastered the level of development reflected in that particular item. In this case, your answer to the test item is a definite 'NO'.

You need not fear that this fails to do justice to the child's abilities. After all, he isn't taking an exam! Remember that the Charts are designed to help you make an initial assessment of the child's level of development in order to inform your subsequent teaching activities. So, in the case of the ability which the child shows only occasionally, this probably means that you have homed in on the critical point of the child's development of that particular skill. Here you will need rather more detailed information about the child's level of functioning before you embark on a particular teaching scheme. In the next chapter, **Looking Closer**, we shall consider ways in which you obtain more detailed information about what the child can and cannot do. But for the present, it is wise to be slightly conservative about the child's abilities. In this way you will avoid the mistake of assuming that the child has mastered skills which, in fact, he has yet to learn.

An overall perspective. By dividing our assessment into various areas of development we are immediately able to gain an overall impression of the child's strengths and weaknesses. It is important here to re-affirm a point which we made in the Introduction to the book: that a handicapped child is not typically evenly delayed in all areas of development. For example, it is not uncommon to find that a young Down's syndrome child has made less progress in his language than in other areas of development; and furthermore, that his ability to use language may not have advanced as much as his ability to understand language.

The Developmental Charts will help to highlight these variations and can direct our teaching efforts to specific areas of the child's learning. However, we do not suggest that teaching activities should be concerned only with those areas in which the child has made least progress. Teaching handicapped children is not simply a matter of remedial teaching. It is just as important to encourage the child's strengths as it is to minimise his weaknesses. But this overall picture of the child is extremely valuable in helping us to organise our educational priorities.

Extra benefits. We have concentrated primarily on the usefulness of the Developmental Charts in making an initial assessment of the child's development. We would like to conclude this section by pointing out some other ways in which you can use the Developmental Charts.

1. The child's future progress

After you have been teaching the child for some time, you may wish to obtain an overall picture of his progress. If so, you can very easily re-assess the child in exactly the same way as you conducted the initial assessment. Of course, we are not suggesting that you should be continuously assessing the child through the Charts. You are a teacher, not a tester. But you may find it useful to assess the child once a term, or once every six months.

If you use the same Charts, but different coloured ink, you will obtain a very clear picture of the progress that the child has made since your initial assessment. This is often very encouraging, particularly during those periods when you may feel that the child is hardly making any progress at all. Moreover, you may find that the profile of the child's strengths and weaknesses has altered since the initial assessment. Thus you can redirect your attention to those areas of development in which the child now requires most help.

2. A Common Language for describing the child's development

Very often you will find yourself in the position of discussing the child's progress with someone else. Sometimes these conversations remain at the level of statements like 'Oh, he's doing fine,' or 'He's a bit behind with his language'. However, there will also be occasions when you are discussing the child with someone who, like you, is directly involved in the child's education—perhaps one of his parents, or his speech therapist, or his physiotherapist.

In these situations, you will want to describe the child's behaviour more specifically, for you will want to decide exactly what you both hope to achieve through your combined teaching activities. The Developmental Charts can help communication here, for they enable you to talk about the child in terms which clearly describe what he can and cannot do. And, of course, the Charts also provide you with a clear framework within which to follow the child's progress with his other teachers.

3. An Introduction to Child Development

Related to the previous point, some of the people who will co-operate with you in furthering the child's education may have only a minimal understanding of child development. The Developmental Charts will help you to explain some of the ideas which are central to teaching the child, for example that the child's progress can be considered under various areas of development and that the child's future learning is dependent on what he has already learned.

Perhaps most important of all, the Charts show just how many steps are involved in learning even very basic skills (indeed, you yourself may have been surprised at the number of steps involved. This was certainly our experience!). The fact that the child has already progressed through some of the stages, however few, shows that he is capable of further learning. Equally, by highlighting the many steps involved in developing a skill, the Charts warn us against placing unrealistic demands on the child.

Summary

In this chapter we have outlined the ways in which the

Developmental Charts can be used to make an initial assessment of the child:

(1) the Charts divide the child's development into five major skill areas;

(2) within each area the Charts outline the sequence of stages which children normally pass through during the first five years of life.

Thus the Charts enable you to form an overall picture of the child's developmental strengths and weaknesses.

In addition, the Charts may be used:

(i) to monitor the child's future progress;

(ii) as a common language for describing the child's development;

(iii) as an introduction to child development.

From your initial assessment of the child you will have become aware of those areas of development in which the child needs most encouragement. In the following chapter, **Looking Closer**, we want to consider how you can obtain more detailed information about the child in order to help you to decide on specific teaching objectives.

2 : Looking Closer

Your initial assessment of the child through the Developmental Charts will have given you an overall picture of his development. From this initial profile, you will have decided upon those areas of development in which you particularly want to help the child, e.g. language development, social skills, eye-hand co-ordination, etc. Thus you have made considerable progress towards deciding on what you are going to teach. The next step is to build up a much more detailed picture of the child's level of functioning in those areas in which you want to help his development.

Possibly, at this stage, you may prefer to move on to specific teaching activities. After all, you may ask, haven't I already found out the child's level of functioning through the Developmental Charts?

Certainly, the Charts do provide an immensely useful initial assessment of the child, but there are two reasons why they do not really give you sufficient information upon which to base a specific teaching scheme.

(1) The charts present only the significant milestones of development. They do not describe every step on the way. To put it differently, the Charts measure development in yards, even miles. Yet development is really a whole series of very small steps which need to be measured in units more like feet and inches. So in order to locate the child's exact position developmentally, and to chart his subsequent progress, we need to use much more sensitive measuring tools than are provided by the Charts. In other words, we have to look a lot closer at what the child can and cannot do.

(2) All the items in the Charts are YES/NO items; you simply decide whether or not the child is functioning at the level indicated by the particular item. Yet behaviour is not an

all-or-nothing affair. It is subject to tremendous variation, and often it is in this area of variation that we learn most, both about the child's current level of development and about his future progress.

In this chapter we want to suggest some ways in which you can obtain more detailed information about the child. We would ask you to bear one thing in mind. The observations are not conducted for their own sake, but rather to guide you in choosing teaching objectives and planning teaching schemes to achieve these objectives. Thus you are looking for specific information for a specific purpose.

How, then, do you go about obtaining this information?

A. DECIDE ON THE ACTIVITY THAT YOU ARE GOING TO OBSERVE

The first step, in planning your observation of the child, is to choose a specific activity to observe. This may seem rather trite, but the accent is on the word 'specific'.

What is a specific activity?

Quite simply, one that you can define in words. So set yourself the task of writing down on paper the activity to be observed. The point of this is that if you cannot describe the activity in words, then it is unlikely that you will be able to observe it objectively.

In many cases you should find little difficulty in defining the activity. For example, with a view to encouraging the child's language development, you may wish to observe:

(i) the number of times he uses words in the context of a particular game;

(ii) the frequency of his utterances in different situations;

(iii) the range of different words that he uses, i.e. the extent of his vocabulary.

Which activity should you choose to observe?

This will depend on what you have already discovered about

B

the child in the course of your initial assessment. For example, you may have noticed that a child will often imitate words spoken by others, but rarely utters words spontaneously. Here you may want to observe (*a*) what words the child imitates, (*b*) what words he uses spontaneously, and (*c*) those situations in which he uses spontaneous language most of all.

These observations will give you first some baseline measures of the child's imitative and spontaneous language. Second, they may give you some clues as to why he does use language spontaneously, e.g. he may be most vocal only when he wants something, such as a drink.

Global impressions
It may not always be easy to define a specific activity that you want to observe. This is often because you are concerned about a general characteristic of the child's behaviour in many different situations, for example, that he is 'naughty' or 'distractable' or that he 'lacks independence'.

These are global impressions of the child and while they may reflect genuine causes for concern, they do not put you in a position to help the child. Instead, try to pinpoint the specific behaviours that give rise to these global impressions. You may find, for example, that your impression of the child's 'naughtiness' derives from the fact that he frequently throws toys and other objects around the room.

Just by translating an overall impression into a specific activity you have made considerable progress. There are now many specific activities and events that you can observe which may give you clues as to why the child throws the toys, and therefore what you can do to change his behaviour:

(*a*) What happens before the child throws the toys? (how long has he been left on his own with the toys? Were you trying to teach him something which was too difficult for him?)

(*b*) What happens after he throws the toys? (does he get most attention from others at this point?)

(c) In what situations does he not throw toys? (This will give you further clues as to why he is 'naughty' on some occasions, but not on others.)

Lastly, remember that by describing the child's activities in clearly defined, observable behaviour, we can measure the success of our teaching schemes by comparing the child's behaviour before teaching with his behaviour once our teaching schemes have been put into practice. In Section 3, we shall have more to say about assessing the effectiveness of our teaching.

B. PLAN THE OBSERVATIONS

Once you have chosen the activity that you are going to observe, the next step is to decide how best to observe it.

You will first have to decide whether or not the activity has to be observed in any one particular situation. There are usually two possible reasons why this may be so:

(a) The activity is restricted to certain situations. For example, observations of the child feeding himself will generally have to be conducted at mealtimes.

(b) The situation has, or may have, a particular influence on the child's behaviour. In a previous example, we referred to the child who throws toys in certain situations, but not in others. Obviously, you will want to find out how these situations vary. Therefore, it will be as important to observe the different situations as it is to observe the child's behaviour.

In both instances it is very important to bear in mind that your job is only to observe, no more and no less. This has two implications:

(i) Make sure that you are not required to do anything else while you are observing the child. If, for example, you intend to observe the child feeding himself, then arrange for someone else to carry out your usual mealtime duties, such as serving food or supervising other children at the table.

(ii) *Observe, don't teach.* As a teacher, it is natural to want to step in and help the child when he gets into difficulties. But if you do so, then you are not really finding out what the child can and cannot do. Remember, in this situation you are a learner, not a teacher.

Selecting the situation

Now let us turn to activities which do not have to be observed in specific situations. Here you can decide for yourself where and when you wish to observe the child. In fact, many of your observations will fall into this category, e.g. observing the child drawing, or building with bricks, or playing with dolls, or looking at picture books. As with the activities which must be observed 'in situ', your objective is to obtain accurate information about the child. But now you can make your task easier by creating your own situation.

It is most important that the situation should be as free as possible from distractions. This will help the child to concentrate on what he is doing and it will also help you to observe him without being disturbed.

Ideally, you should observe the child in a separate room and at a time when there will be no noise outside the room. If you cannot arrange for a separate room, you can still create an observation area in the classroom by using screens, or a Wendy house. In fact, screens can be very useful if you want to observe the child without letting him know that you are looking on.

Finally, remember that the child may also be distracted as much by irrelevant objects as by other people. So make sure that your observation area contains only those toys and materials which are necessary for the activity that you want to observe.

C. KEEP A RECORD OF THE ACTIVITY

You will have put much thought into deciding on a specific activity to observe and how to observe it. All this preparation will prove worthwhile only if you keep an accurate record of your observations. The record will not only tell you what the child can do now, but it will provide the most objective yardstick against which to measure his future progress.

However, we appreciate that record-keeping can be somewhat burdensome if carried to extremes. The approach that we have adopted is to pre-plan our record-keeping in such a way as to provide us with the maximum of relevant information with the minimum of effort. We find that this is most easily achieved by preparing checklists which can be filled in very simply while we are observing the child. The design of each checklist depends on the way in which we wish to measure the particular activity. So we would now like to consider the most useful measures of the child's activity, and the types of checklists which we could use to record these measures.

Measuring the child's behaviour

1. Frequency

This is perhaps the simplest method of observing and measuring behaviour. All you do is keep a count of the number of times the child displays the behaviour over a given period of time.

Frequency counts can be used when the behaviour is in the form of separate units or events. One example of such behaviour is spoken language. Suppose, for example, that the child you observe is at the level of using one or two clear words. You may want to expand the range of the child's vocabulary. But first it may be more appropriate to encourage the child to make more use of the words which he can already say. Therefore you will need to find out how often the child actually uses words at present.

A frequency count gives you a baseline measure of the child's use of language. Furthermore, subsequent frequency counts will tell you how much progress the child has made in his use of language.

Frequency checklist. Figure 2 shows a very simple checklist for noting the frequency of a child's use of words during different play activities. We had already decided on the play activities prior to the observation session and how long we would spend on each activity. Thus all the observer had to do was to tick in the appropriate box each time that the child said a word.

NAME: *Fred*   DATE: *23rd March*

Activity	Words Used	Time
Picture book	1111 11	2 min.
Trigger-Jigger	1111	2 min.
Form-board	11	2 min.
Doll Play	111	2 min.
Pop-In	1111 111	2 min.

Figure 2. Frequency of words used during different play activities

2. Duration

Many activities do not take the form of separate events and therefore cannot easily be measured by frequency counts. Take the example of a child looking at a picture book. This is a far more continuous activity than the single-word utterances to which we referred previously. So it would be more appropriate to record the length of time the child spends looking at the book.

As with frequency counts, the duration of an activity also gives you a baseline measure of the child's level of functioning against which you can measure his subsequent progress.

The slower learning of many handicapped children is often attributed, at least in part, to their extreme distractability, or their inability to concentrate on a particular activity for any length of time. Therefore, the duration of a child's activity can often provide a useful measure of his development, even in cases of activities which can also be measured by frequency counts, e.g. stacking bricks or threading beads.

Duration checklist. Figure 3 shows a checklist for noting the length of time that the child spends playing with any one toy. The toys were selected prior to the observation session, and were presented singly to the child for three minutes each. The observer, with the help of a stop-watch, simply noted in the 'In' column, the length of time the child spent playing with each toy.

NAME: *Doreen*   DATE: *6th June*

Activity	Total Time	Time In (secs.)	Total Time In
Car	3 min.	10, 23, 14, 2, 17	66 secs.
Ringstack	3 min.	18, 7, 4	29 secs.
Picture book	3 min.	12, 16, 4, 8	40 secs.
Marble Run	3 min.	6, 17, 36, 39, 25	123 secs.

Figure 3. Time spent in different play activities

Note: The previous examples have referred to activities which we wish to encourage in the child. But frequency and duration can also be used to observe and measure behaviour which we may wish to discourage, e.g. disruptive behaviours, head-banging, crying or bed-wetting.

Often, our attempts to eliminate such behaviours will not meet with total success immediately. But if we are able to detect a reduction in the frequency or the duration of such behaviours, then we can feel more confident that our teaching schemes are proving effective and should, in time, succeed in eliminating the undesirable behaviours completely.

3. Variety
Developmental progress may not always be represented in either the frequency or duration of an activity, but rather in its

variety. Consider, for example, a skill which we as adults tend to take for granted—reaching out and grasping an object. Many handicapped children, in particular very young ones, acquire this form of eye-hand co-ordination only very gradually.

But even when a child can reach in front of him to pick up a matchbox, we may be premature in considering his reaching and grasping skills to be complete. For example, is he as successful when the matchbox is placed to his left, or his right, high up or low down? Is his grasp as skilful when picking up a marble, or a handkerchief, or a doll, or a piece of string?

Variety checklist. Figure 4 shows a checklist for recording the number of times the child reaches towards a dangling toy which is presented to the child in a variety of positions. The observer simply ticks, in the appropriate box, each time that the child reaches towards the toy when presented.

NAME: *James*   DATE: *29th January*

Toy presented four times in each position	
Position	*Reach*
Middle	✓ ✓ ✓ ✓
Upper Left	✓ ✓
Upper Right	✓ ✓ ✓
Lower Left	
Lower Right	✓

Figure 4. Reaching for toy in varied positions

Note: Asking about the variety of behaviour also raises the important point that development is not merely a 'vertical' progression to higher levels of functioning, but it also shows itself in a 'horizontal' expansion of activities. We must therefore be wary of over-emphasising the child's 'vertical' development at the expense of broadening and consolidating those skills which he has already learned.

Thus far we have concentrated on

(*a*) the choice of activity;

(*b*) the planning of your observations;

(*c*) methods of recording in terms of (i) frequency, (ii) duration or (iii) variety.

Analysing skills

We would now like to introduce you to a rather different and, in some ways, a more detailed approach to observing the child's activity. The basic rationale which underlies this approach is that very many activities or skills are, in fact, made up of a number of separate actions, or sub-skills.

Take the example of driving a car. This requires many sub-skills, such as manipulating the steering wheel, operating the foot pedals, estimating speed and distance, interpreting road-signs and so on. We can all probably remember just how hard it was at first to master all these sub-skills before we combined them into reasonably competent driving. So we can well understand the problems faced by someone who has just started learning to drive.

However, there are many other skills, such as using a knife and fork, or putting on a coat, which we have so thoroughly mastered that we tend to forget how difficult it was to learn them initially. Thus we are likely to overlook all the steps involved.

Yet this knowledge is vital if we are to be effective teachers. In the case of children who have difficulties in learning, it is especially important that we do not frustrate them by expecting them to learn too many things at once. We can make sure that we are not placing too many demands on the child by using the method of Skills Analysis.

Skills Analysis. Skills Analysis helps us to set out all the necessary skills involved in a particular activity. Let us take a concrete example—building a tower of bricks. An analysis of this activity yields the following skills:

(1) looking at and focusing on one of the bricks;

(2) reaching out accurately for the brick;

B*

(3) grasping the brick—typically between finger(s) and thumb;

(4) picking up the brick;

(5) placing the brick on top of another brick with the sides correctly aligned;

(6) letting go of the brick without disturbing the 'tower';

(7) looking for another brick and repeating all the previous steps.

Once you have made such an analysis your teaching is helped in the following ways:

(1) You can find out exactly which of the various steps the child can do and which he cannot. Hence you can find out which skills the child has mastered and which he has yet to learn. Figure 5 shows a checklist for observing all the steps involved in making a tower of five bricks. The observer simply places a tick against each completed step. Note the series of columns on the checklist. This is so that the observer can record the child's repeated attempts at this task. This minimises the possibility of interpreting one chance success as evidence that the child had really mastered that step.

NAME: Christopher		DATE: 12th May		
1. Look at brick	√	√	√	√
2. Reach for brick	√	√	√	√
3. Grasp brick	√	√	√	√
4. Pick up brick	√	√	√	√
5. Place brick	×	×	√	×
6. Let go brick	×	×	√	×
7. Search for other brick	√	√	√	√

Figure 5. Analysis of building a tower

(2) You can avoid the mistake of attempting to teach the child too many things at the same time. By analysing the activity into specific steps and skills, it is now much easier to plan what to teach the child.

(3) You can observe the progress that the child is making, even before he has mastered the whole activity. Suppose, for argument, that the child was initially capable only of the first two steps, looking at and reaching for the brick. You then taught him to grasp and pick up a brick. Now, even though he cannot as yet stack bricks, you have the satisfaction of knowing that he is progressing toward this final objective.

Finally, we would like to point out that Skills Analysis is not applicable merely to sequential activities, like building a tower of bricks, or feeding or dressing, where many steps are involved. Even in activities which involve only one step, for example, when a child says 'cup', many skills are required.

In our book *Let Me Speak*, we have dealt extensively with the skills necessary for appropriate language. Similarly, the skills required for many other activities are considered in our other book, *Let Me Play*.

It is absolutely essential that you understand how many skills are involved in learning any new activity. This will help to guide your observations, and it will also help you to avoid placing too many demands on the child whom you are teaching.

Environmental influences

Thus far we have considered different ways of measuring and recording the child's activity. However, no activity occurs in a vacuum. Therefore we may also want to learn more about the context in which the activity occurs. In doing so, we may learn more about the activity itself; but, more specifically, we may uncover some vital clues as to the factors which may influence the activity. This information will be extremely useful when we design our subsequent teaching schemes.

What sort of questions can we ask about the context of a particular activity?

1. When and where does the activity occur most?
This is the most immediate and obvious question that we can ask about the context of a particular activity. As the question

implies, many of the child's activities may be variably influenced by different situations. For instance, he may vocalise
much more in the bathroom than in another room. By contrasting the two situations, we may be able to determine those
factors which have most influence on the activity.

Recording. We can use the checklists which we have already
described for measuring the child's behaviour. But now we must
keep a separate checklist for each different time and place that
we observe the child.

Once we have recorded when and where the activity occurs,
or occurs most, we can then go on to more specific questions:

2. *What materials are present?*

Very often, the activity may be crucially influenced by the
materials, or toys, which may be present in the situation. For
example, a child's reaching or grasping may be differentially
affected by the physical appearance of toys, e.g. their shape,
colour and texture; or by whether they are mobile or static; or
by whether they produce specific effects, such as musical notes
or flashing lights.

By focusing on the materials which influence the child's
activity, we can learn a lot not only about the child's abilities
but also about his interests and preferences. Both kinds of
information will prove useful in our subsequent teaching
schemes.

Recording. All the checklists which we have described for
measuring the child's behaviour can be used to record his
activity with different toys and materials.

3. *Who else is present?*

Sometimes we find that a child enjoys an activity most of all
when he is in the company of one particular person. The
'favoured one' could be his mother, or his father, or his school-
teacher, or perhaps an older brother or sister. It may well be
that the child is especially fond of this other person, in which

case it can be very helpful to involve him or her in teaching the child, whenever this is practicable.

But it is equally important to ask why the child enjoys the company of this one person in particular. It may be related to the way that he or she plays with the child. If so, we can apply this knowledge to our own teaching methods. However, this is a topic which we shall consider in much greater depth in Chapter 9, page 137.

Methods of recording

Finally, we want to review various methods which you can use to record your observations.

(i) *Checklists.* We hope that you will agree that all the checklists which we have discussed are very easy to complete. This is because each one was designed to serve a specific function. This, in turn, was made possible by deciding beforehand exactly what we wanted to observe. Similarly, with proper planning you should find little difficulty in designing checklists to meet your own observation requirements.

By deciding on what you want to observe and by using properly constructed checklists, much of your recording can be carried out as the behaviour occurs.

(ii) *Aids to recording.* There will be occasions, however, when you will not be able to keep an ongoing record of the child's activity. This may be, for example, because the activity occurs too quickly for on-the-spot records, as say, in the child's use of expressive language.

In such situations it is best to make a tape recording of the whole observation session. Later, you can replay the recording to extract the particular information that you require.

We have used two special aids in recording our observations of the child:

(a) *Video-tape recording.* VTR has the advantage that you can make both a visual and an auditory record of the child's activity. Therefore you can record almost any activity by means of VTR.

However, VTR equipment is very expensive and may well be beyond the budget of most schools. If your school does not have a VTR, it may be possible to borrow a set from another local educational establishment, such as a college of education.

It is well worth enquiring about such possibilities, because VTR is useful not only in your initial observation of the child, but also in assessing the effectiveness of your teaching schemes. In Section 3, we discuss the latter use of VTR more fully.

(b) *Audio-cassette recording.* Cassette recorders are restricted to sound recordings. In this sense they are less versatile than VTR equipment.

However, cassette recorders do have certain advantages:

(1) Unlike VTR equipment, they can be easily concealed, thus avoiding the possibility of distracting the child during your observation session. But do make sure that the microphone is close enough to record what is being said, either by you or by the child.

(2) Cassette recorders are obviously very useful in recording language activities and, indeed, this is probably their prime function. However, you can also use them to make a 'running commentary' of the child's non-linguistic activities. You do not need to be an expert to use the recorder in this way. Once you have decided on what you want to describe, it is usually quite easy to devise a verbal 'shorthand' for it. For example, if you want to obtain a record of the length of time that the child spends playing with a toy, you need simply say 'start with teddy' when he begins playing and 'stop with teddy' when he abandons the toy.

(3) Sometimes you may wish to obtain a record of the child's activity at home, rather than at school. It will not often be easy for his parents to take a VTR home, but you can reasonably ask them to make a cassette recording. Many

of the parents who have worked with us have made excellent recordings of their child's activity in the home. This can be particularly informative when you wish to compare the child's behaviour at home with his behaviour at school.

(4) Lastly, cassette recorders are very inexpensive nowadays. If you or your school can possibly afford to buy one, we believe that it will prove well worth the money.

Summary

In this chapter we have suggested how you can obtain detailed observations of what the child can and cannot do:

A. Decide on the activity that you are going to observe;
B. Plan the observation situation;
C. Keep a record of the activity.

We described three ways of measuring and recording the child's behaviour:

(1) Frequency
(2) Duration
(3) Variety.

We then introduced an alternative and more detailed approach to observing the child: *Skills Analysis*.

In addition we stressed the importance of considering the *Environmental influences* on the child's activity:

(1) When and where does the activity occur most?
(2) What materials are present?
(3) Who else is present?

Finally, we reviewed *Methods of Recording*:

(i) Checklists;
(ii) Aids to recording (*a*) video-tape recorders (*b*) audio-cassette recorders.

We hope that by now you will be well aware of the different ways of looking closer at the child's activity. Perhaps we have been too successful! Your head may be swimming with all the points to bear in mind when observing the child. And, you may be wondering, 'Isn't all this too much to think of at once?'

You're quite right. We certainly wouldn't advise you even to try. The truth of the matter is, of course, that only some of the previous points will be relevant to the observation of any one particular activity. Our purpose in this chapter has been to give you some ideas of what to look for when observing the child. But we would also stress again that your observations have a specific purpose. This is to find out exactly what the child can and cannot do at the present time. Once you have found this out you are in a position to decide on an appropriate teaching objective for him. This is our subject for the next chapter.

3 : The Teaching Objective

WHAT IS A TEACHING OBJECTIVE?

Initially, we can state that a teaching objective describes what the child should be able to do after undergoing the educational experiences which you provide for him.

But in this chapter, we want to develop a much more exact definition of a teaching objective. In framing this definition we have in mind three functions which the teaching objective should serve:

(1) it should tell you exactly what your teaching should achieve;
(2) it should help you to design particular teaching schemes for the child concerned;
(3) it should allow you to tell whether or not your teaching is effective.

Now let us consider what are the characteristics of a teaching objective which will serve these three functions.

A. The teaching objective refers to the activity of the child

Let us note first of all that the teaching objective refers to what you expect the *child* to do. It does not refer to your own activity. In effect, the teaching objective refers to what should be the successful outcome of your teaching activity. The point is that, however carefully you prepare and execute your teaching activity, your only criterion of success is whether it actually helps the child's learning.

B. The teaching objective refers to a specific observable activity

This is very important. Indeed, we consider it to be the

essential characteristic of the teaching objective. We can best illustrate what we mean by describing a teaching objective which we chose for a little girl, Carol, who was brought to see us.

Her mother was particularly concerned that Carol used very little speech. From our own observations of the child, we also noticed that, although in many ways her development was very promising, she hardly used any words in communicating with others. We therefore decided that our aim would be to encourage Carol's use of expressive language. However, this was our overall aim—it was not a specific objective.

After assessing the extent of Carol's development of expressive language, we then decided on what we believed was a correct teaching objective for Carol. This was that she should use the appropriate nouns in referring to three objects: a cup, a spoon, and a ball.

We actually taught Carol to use these words in the context of a 'posting-box' game, in which she was required to name each object before she was allowed to 'post' it (see *Let Me Speak*, page 82). Carol's mother also played this game with her at home.

Now the reason why we chose this particular teaching objective need not concern us here. Instead, we would like to point out the benefits of such a specific, observable teaching objective.

1. The teaching objective helps us to structure our teaching activity
Once we knew what we specifically wanted to achieve, we were able to devise an appropriate teaching game which focused only on Carol's use of the three 'target' words, cup, spoon and ball. Had we simply acted with the general aim of improving Carol's expressive language development, it is far less likely that we would have decided on a particular teaching activity which would have been appropriate for Carol. We would probably have made the mistake of asking Carol to name too many different objects at once. But by having a finite, specific teaching objective, we were able to help Carol's learning. In

addition, such a teaching objective made our task as teachers much more manageable.

2. The teaching objective helps us to monitor the child's progress
By defining our teaching objective in terms of observable behaviour, we were in a position to judge whether or not Carol was making any progress in her use of words. Specifically, over the successive days on which this game was played, we noted the number of times that Carol correctly used the words to refer to the particular objects. This information not only provided us with a record of Carol's progress, but it also showed us whether or not our teaching was proving successful.

Furthermore, we were able to pinpoint any specific difficulties as they arose. For example, although Carol generally increased her appropriate use of the nouns as we played this game, she did not say 'cup' as easily as the other two words. This directed us to modify the game to give Carol extra help in using the word 'cup' appropriately.

Finally, the advantage of a clearly defined, observable teaching objective is that we are in no doubt when the objective has been achieved. Apart from the obvious satisfaction that this brings, it is also our cue to move on to fresh teaching objectives.

3. The teaching objective helps us to discuss the child's progress with other teachers
In the Introduction to the book we argued that it is increasingly likely that more than one teacher will be involved in the development of a handicapped child. These teachers could actually be several teachers at the child's school, but they could also include the health visitor, the speech therapist, the physiotherapist, the nursery nurse or the child's parents. Very often, these different teachers will not see the child at the same time or in the same situation. Yet, unless they co-ordinate their activities, the benefit to the child's learning may be diminished and in certain circumstances, actually impeded.

It is very important, therefore, that each teacher understands very clearly what another teacher may be trying to teach. This is where an unambiguously stated teaching objective proves so useful. Just as the previous points have shown how the teaching objective helps to clarify our own thinking about what to teach an individual child, it is also ideal for communicating our intentions to others. Of course, the best form of co-ordination is for all the child's teachers to plan their teaching objectives together. This ensures that the right hand really does know what the left hand is doing.

We may add that the teaching objective also enables us to discuss the child's progress objectively with other teachers. This is a topic to which we shall return in Chapter 11.

C. The teaching objective refers to an activity which the child should be able to demonstrate in the near, rather than the distant, future

What do we mean by the near future? There can be no fixed answer to this question, as different teaching objectives will vary in the degree of difficulty they present to the learner and because different children will vary in their speed of learning particular skills. However, a useful rule of thumb is to choose a teaching objective which can be achieved in a matter of days or weeks, rather than months.

One very important guideline is to remember that all new learning depends on what the learner is capable of at the present time. So, before you decide on a specific teaching objective for any particular child, you must find out what the child's level of functioning actually is. This will involve observation and assessment of the child, topics which have been considered in greater detail in the two previous chapters.

However, a simple illustration of what we mean by the near future may be given by returning to the previous example of our teaching objective for Carol. This was to be able to use the correct word in referring to three objects, a cup, a spoon and a ball. The point we wish to make here is that we decided upon this objective only *after* we had observed Carol over a period of time.

Our observations told us that Carol used hardly any words in communicating with others. Thus it was relevant to choose a teaching objective which would help her to be able to express herself. But our observations also told us that Carol did vocalise frequently, without necessarily being understood, and that she did occasionally utter a meaningful word (Mama). Furthermore, we also observed that Carol did understand the meaning of many words when spoken by others (including the words 'cup', 'spoon' and 'ball'). We therefore surmised that the next step for Carol was to begin to use a few words appropriately. It was only at this stage that we decided on the specific teaching objective which we described earlier.

Now, if our observations had shown that Carol hardly ever made any utterances of any kind, then a more appropriate short-term teaching objective would have been, for example, to increase the frequency of her vocalisations. Only when this was achieved would we go on to encourage Carol to learn to use specific words.

Why is it important to have short-term teaching objectives? Remember the third function which the teaching objective should serve: that it should tell you whether or not your teaching is being effective.

If the teaching objective were a long-term one, requiring several months before you could expect to achieve it, you would have to wait a very long time before you found out whether or not your teaching had been effective. By contrast, a short-term objective provides you with this information much more quickly. This has two advantages:

(1) If your teaching has been successful, i.e. the objective has been achieved, this is very encouraging in itself. Furthermore, it tells you that you can now move on to a further teaching objective.

(2) If the teaching objective has not been achieved, or if the child is not making any progress toward it, then this is your signal to re-appraise the situation. You may decide that the teaching objective was either inappropriate or,

more likely, rather too difficult for the child. Alternatively, you may decide that the teaching objective was correctly chosen but that it was the particular method of teaching which was inappropriate for this particular child. In this case you would devise new ways to help the child to achieve the skill described in the teaching objective.

In either case you have not lost much time. Thus a short-term teaching objective allows you to keep a much more effective check on the child's progress, and thereby on the usefulness of your teaching.

D. The teaching objective refers to the conditions under which the activity should occur

We have emphasised the importance of describing a teaching objective in terms of a specific observable activity. In addition we need to state, with equal clarity, the conditions under which we expect the activity to occur.

In order to illustrate how such conditions can vary and why it is important that we recognise these variations, we would like to return to our teaching objective for Carol. This was that she should use the appropriate noun when referring to a cup, a ball and a spoon. Restricting ourselves to the spoon, for the moment, here are some different conditions under which we might want Carol to say the word 'spoon':

(1) teacher holds up spoon, says 'spoon'; Carol says 'spoon';
(2) teacher holds up spoon; Carol says 'spoon';
(3) teacher holds up picture of spoon; Carol says 'spoon'.

These are just three conditions under which Carol might say 'spoon'. Undoubtedly you can think of several more, but the previous examples will serve to point out why we consider it necessary to include a clear statement of the conditions for an action in your description of a teaching objective.

It will be evident that the demand placed on Carol, that of saying 'spoon', varies in difficulty according to the different conditions mentioned previously. In *Condition 1*, the teacher holds up a spoon and provides Carol with a verbal model of the word 'spoon'. Yet in *Condition 2*, no such model is provided—the teacher merely holds up a spoon. Thus Carol's task is harder because she has to remember that 'spoon' is the correct word for this object. Similarly, Carol's task becomes harder still in *Condition 3*, because she has to be able to recognise that the picture in front of her represents a spoon.

Each of these different conditions requires Carol to have developed particular skills in order to be able to say the word 'spoon'. Thus the choice of any one of these conditions for a teaching objective will depend on Carol's current level of language development. We may also note a further point, which is inherent in the notion that different conditions can affect the difficulty of the child's learning task. This is that a child's progress is not always shown by new actions, but by the same actions under more demanding conditions. Thus the grading of conditions could represent a series of teaching objectives for the child.

Summary

We began this section with a provisional definition of a teaching objective. We can now provide a much more exact definition by summarising the previous points.

The teaching objective describes:

(*a*) the activity of the child;
(*b*) a specific observable activity;
(*c*) an activity which the child should be able to demonstrate in the near, rather than the distant, future;
(*d*) the conditions under which the activity should occur.

Once you have decided upon your teaching objective, you will then have to consider how you can help the child to achieve it. We move on to this subject in Section 2.

SECTION 2: HELPING A CHILD TO LEARN

Introduction

In the previous section we outlined the essential preparation which is required before we can hope to help a child to learn— for instance, taking time to assess what the child already knows, choosing an appropriate teaching objective and breaking down each task into its component sub-skills.

However, this essential preparation is only part of the story. An equally essential part of teaching lies in actually getting the message across so that the child himself learns what we planned so carefully to teach him. This is sometimes called the art of teaching. However, although some teachers may appear to be naturally gifted in this direction, this art can be learned. That is what this section is about. Guidelines will be given on how to clear away obstacles which may lie in the path of progress, and ways in which we can produce favourable conditions for learning.

Teaching games
In our 'Let Me' books, we have given plenty of specific ideas on how a teacher can help a child to learn. We have presented learning tasks in the context of structured teaching games which a teacher can adapt to meet the needs of individual children.

But why this emphasis on games and play? Normal children rapidly develop an amazing repertoire of skills in the first five years of life, without an adult consciously sitting down to teach them. One of the most productive ways of learning these basic skills appears to be through the medium of independent exploratory play. The greater the encouragement of such play, the more rapid the child's development.

One of the characteristics of handicapped children is that they have failed to develop these skills in this manner. In fact, some handicapped children (though not all) show little inclination to play on their own, or get stuck at a primitive form of repetitive play or self-stimulation which does not lead to progress.

In our teaching schemes, instead of abandoning the idea of play as a medium for learning, we have suggested ways in which play can be structured so that children can not only learn *through* play, but also learn *how* to play.

One of the encouraging outcomes of this method is that many handicapped children will gradually begin to indulge in spontaneous play outside the teaching sessions, and so begin to practice and develop their emerging skills independently.

However, the problem facing the teacher is to choose the activities that are best suited to help the child's learning, and then to carry them out in the most effective way. The whole of this section is aimed at helping you to become increasingly effective in promoting a child's learning through teaching games. We have divided the section into four chapters.

Chapter 4. Individual Differences
This chapter is concerned with catering for individual differences in children. No two children present precisely the same problem. Each child has a unique pattern of strengths and weaknesses, likes and dislikes.

In this chapter we have suggested ways in which these can be taken into account in planning your teaching. Especial reference is made to children with additional handicaps.

Chapter 5. Creating Favourable Conditions
This chapter discusses the creation of favourable physical conditions for learning. It is concerned with the organisation and planning of available time, space and personnel, as well as with the choice of toys and equipment.

Chapter 6. Teaching Skills
As well as general guidelines towards effective teaching, we have described in detail some specific teaching techniques in the context of a variety of teaching situations.

Although based on common sense, the effectiveness of these techniques depends upon their precise and rigorous translation into practice.

Chapter 7. Learning through Spontaneous Play

The aim of the structured teaching games described in this book is to promote the basic skills necessary for independent activity. In spontaneous play, for instance, a child has not only an opportunity to practice and consolidate the skills he has been taught, he can also combine these in new ways and thus develop new skills. This chapter will suggest how teachers can encourage the emergence of spontaneous play.

4 : Individual Differences

INTRODUCTION

Having completed a developmental chart and observed each child in different situations and referred to his case notes, you will be increasingly aware of individual differences.

This chapter is concerned with planning for the individual child; taking into account his strengths and weaknesses. Ways in which a child's strengths can be used to overcome his weaknesses are outlined in the first part of this chapter.

The second part of this chapter is concerned with children with additional sensory defects. The importance of early identification of these handicaps is underlined so that expert advice can be obtained. The use of alternative channels to compensate for irremedial sensory defects is also described.

The third part of this chapter is concerned with the problems posed by the physically handicapped child. Ways in which learning experiences can be adapted for these children are outlined.

The next part of the chapter deals with children's individual preferences and interests and how these can be used to promote their learning.

Lastly, we suggest ways in which a teacher can take her own talents into account and make full use of them in her teaching.

We shall begin by concentrating on a child's strengths and how these can be used to help overcome his weaknesses.

1. Using a child's strengths to overcome his weaknesses

We are often only too well aware of a child's deficiencies, or what he CANNOT do. Reports on individual children are often couched in terms of deficiencies, i.e. he is *not* toilet trained; cannot understand simple commands or feed himself.

It is, of course, important to take these deficiencies into account when planning for the individual child. They will give us some idea of the nature of the provisions we must make: the staff ratio and so on. Where he cannot help himself he will need sufficient staff at hand to help him until he learns to be more independent.

However, before we can give a child effective help, we need a more positive orientation. We need to pay attention to what each child CAN do. All future learning rests on the foundations of past skills (see Section 1).

More important, by concentrating on a child's strengths you can start to help him to overcome his weaknesses.

It is useful to draw up a profile of a child's development so as to highlight his particular strengths.

We shall give you an example of a profile of a single child, Jane, and describe how this technique was used as the basis for language facilitation. Jane was eight years old at the time, and Figure 6 is a profile of her abilities as assessed by psychological tests. (N.B. A similar sort of profile can be derived from the Developmental Charts.)

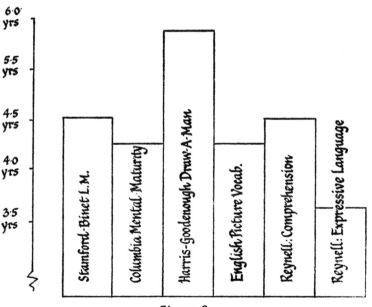

Figure 6

This comprehensive battery of tests highlighted one of Jane's comparative strengths, which was her ability in the Draw-a-man Test. Her mental age on this test was estimated to be five and a quarter. But the profile also highlighted one of her comparative weaknesses: her lack of expressive language. Her 'age' on the expressive language scale of the Reynell Test was just over three and a half. However, her Comprehension was at the four-and-a-half age level, which was commensurate with her general intelligence.

This profile 'would seem to suggest that an appropriate teaching priority for Jane would be her expressive language, and that her ability to draw might be used to facilitate this.

However, before planning a programme for Jane, it was important to look a little more closely at her language abilities. Figure 7 shows the results of a closer analysis of Jane's language, obtained with the Illinois Test of Psycholinguistic Abilities. This profile dramatically highlights two more of Jane's strong points. Although her ability to express herself in language is only at a three-and-a-half-year-old level, her ability to express herself manually (through mime and gesture) is as good as that of a child of six and three quarters.

Similarly, her reception of visual information is up to the five-and-a-half-year-old level.

Before a detailed teaching programme could be evolved, it was important to obtain further details of Jane's language performance in the classroom.

Tape recordings were made, over a period, of Jane's language when she was allowed to play with some novel and interesting toys, and further analysis was made of the results.

Typically Jane is using very short phrases or sentences (94%

	% Phrase Length		% Nouns	% Verbs
	3 words or less	*4 or more words*		
Play Period	94	6	85	15

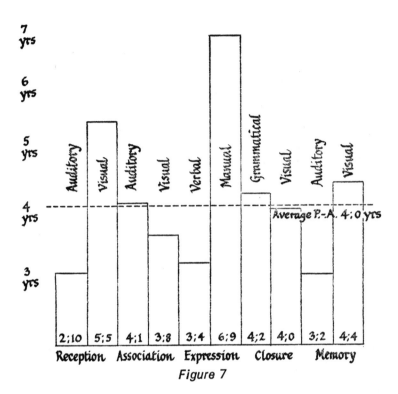

Figure 7

of her phrases are three words long or less). Further analysis of this speech sample shows that Jane's use of language is immature in other ways. That is, she is predominantly using her spoken language as a labelling device. The ratio of nouns to verbs is 85% to 15%.

However, Jane is not merely being repetitive in her spoken language, for she uses a reasonable number of different words.

We were now in a position to describe Jane's assets in some detail in order to make use of these to help her overcome some of her language deficiencies:

c

A summary of Jane's strong points
  (1) expressing herself through mime and gesture;
  (2) drawing;
  (3) extracting information from pictures;
  (4) comprehension of spoken language commensurate with her mental age;
  (5) use of a varied vocabulary.

A summary of Jane's immature use of language
  (1) use of very short phrases, mostly under three words in length;
  (2) incomplete phrases with functional words omitted (telegraphese);
  (3) a preponderance of nouns over verbs;
  (4) a reluctance to use spoken language, and a preference for mime and gesture.

On the basis of this detailed information a series of play situations were devised with specific language teaching objectives as follows:

  (1) to increase Jane's use of different parts of speech, particularly verbs;
  (2) to encourage longer phrases and sentences.

The following account illustrates how Jane's strengths were used to bring about improvement in three different situations as follows:

1. Encouraging greater use of verbs

A series of action pictures was prepared, showing people eating, playing cello, etc. Jane mimed the actions shown in each picture, and then told the teacher what she was doing. The teacher then mimed the actions and Jane had to guess what the teacher was doing. In this situation Jane's ability to use expressive mime and gesture, and her ability to extract information from pictures, encouraged her use of verbs.

Tape recordings were made of all the sessions and an analysis of Jane's language showed that the proportion of verbs used had gone up to 43% as compared with her initial 15%.

2. Encouraging longer sentences

(a) *Using Jane's ability to draw.* Jane was given a large sheet of paper and some crayons, and encouraged to draw and to describe what she was drawing to an interested teacher.

In order to be explicit, she was soon using far longer phrases; 49% of her phrases were over four words in length, as compared with an initial 6%.

(b) *Using Jane's interest in pictures.* In this case the teacher sat next to Jane and drew the pictures. Jane was encouraged to describe what the teacher was drawing. Not only was she soon using longer phrases, but she was also using more nouns, as you can see in the summary table below.

(c) *Picture stories.* Lastly, a sheet of pictures was prepared which were designed to suggest a story. Jane had to name the single character in the story, and then the teacher encouraged her to go on with the story by drawing attention to the other elements in the picture.

This was a very successful way of increasing sentence length, as you can see; 71% of Jane's phrases were now over three words long and some were as many as eight words long.

The table overleaf summarises the result of all these sessions.

We have described in detail one example of the successful use of a child's strong points and how these were used to help overcome some of the weaknesses in the language area.

Most children will co-operate when asked to do something they can do well, and then, with the teacher's help, they can begin to acquire new skills without undue stress.

The example we have given was of a child with considerable abilities. However, the same approach can be used when dealing with a very immature child and even with a child with sensory and motor handicaps. A child's ability to react to flashing lights, for instance, can lead him to acquiring skills in handling and assembling constructional toys, as we have described in *Let Me Play* (page 120).

EFFECTS OF DIFFERENT TEACHING STYLES ON JANE'S
LENGTH OF UTTERANCE AND NOUN-VERB RATIO

	Phrase length %		Nouns %	Verbs %
	3—	4+		
(1) Free play (before teaching)	94	6	85	15
(2) Action pictures	87	13	57	43
(3) Child draws	51	49	72	28
(4) Experimenter draws	65	35	62	38
(5) Picture Stories	29	71	73	27

2. Sensory deficits

Early detection. Many of the children we teach will have some
form of sensory defect. If a sensory defect is suspected, it is
vitally important to seek appropriate professional aid. Even a
slight hearing loss in the early years can delay language
development considerably. As well as treating the child, an
audiologist will be able to tell you where to stand or how to
enunciate so that the child can make out what you are saying.
A very bright child can be developmentally delayed owing to
an untreated hearing defect. A slow-learning child is even more
handicapped.

And a one-off visit to an audiologist is simply not sufficient.
Many handicapped children are prone to catarrh, as well as ear
infections. This often results in a fluctuating hearing loss which
may greatly add to the initial difficulty in acquiring language.

Unhappily, there are still far too many cases reported of
sensory defects which have gone on undetected for years, to the
great detriment of the children in question.

Here is where the teacher's vigilance is of the utmost importance in detecting sensory defects and eliciting professional help.

In our experience, no professional worth his salt will take the teacher to task if she is proved wrong. He would rather spend some time assessing children who turn out not to have any defect, than be faced with older children whose defect has remained undetected.

It is important to seek the advice of speech therapists also, especially when specific defects are suspected in the speech area. The skills of speech therapists and those of teachers often overlap. The best results are obtained when teachers and therapists can work together.

Alternative channels. As well as seeking expert advice, it may be necessary for a teacher to bypass a child's sensory defect and to find alternative ways of helping him to learn. We cannot wait until a deaf or partially-hearing child has learnt to lip-read before establishing some form of communication with him. Much of a child's learning depends upon communication, and if he is not able to hear us we may have to set up a means of non-verbal communication with him in order to help him to learn. A sign system, such as a simplified Paget/Gorman system, when linked with the spoken language, will also help him learn to understand and use spoken language eventually, and it will at least tide him over until he does. A child who cannot make himself understood can be very frustrated.

Similarly, a very large proportion of children in ESN(S) schools suffer from some degree of visual defect. It is not easy to test an immature child's sight, although there are opthalmic surgeons who specialise in this, so many minor defects may go undetected without the teacher's vigilance. Nor is it easy to get a retarded infant to wear glasses, as many teachers and parents will realise to their cost. In some cases the child's eyesight may be so badly affected that he is unable to learn through looking at things. Yet he still needs the experience which other children gain through examining objects and looking at pictures. His 'looking' may have to be done with his fingers. A good teacher will help him to compensate for his lack of vision. The first picture book of familiar objects (see *Let Me Speak*, page 67) may have to be made by using a variety of textures instead of colours. The 'picture' of the teddy bear may have to be cut out of teddy bear cloth with shiny eyes added. And by using junk material and glue, pictures can be built up to give a 3-D effect so that children can feel the shape of the object as well as the different textures. Partially sighted children are also helped by being given auditory cues. A child will be helped in his recognition of familiar toys if they each have a characteristic sound. Some suitable toys can be bought: squeaking toys, musical toys, and so on. You could also invest in a stock of different-sized bells, and these could be firmly attached to the child's toys. Shops selling oriental goods are useful places to find bells with different pitches. A child can even learn to catch a ball he cannot see, if it has a bell inside and he can 'hear' it coming. (See *Let Me Play*, catching balls, page 91.)

3. Physical handicap

Seeking professional help. A severely cerebral palsied child may become very frustrated because he has not the fine motor control necessary to put his ideas into practice. The bricks he is trying to stack may fly all over the place, or his paint brush may refuse to obey him. It is important to seek expert advice from a physiotherapist in this case. She will be able to suggest the best position to put the child in to enable him to have the maximum control of his hands. She will also be able to suggest how wedges and other aids can be used to support the child lying, sitting or standing.

Ideally, the teacher and therapist need to work in close co-operation in the education of physically handicapped children. The dividing line between physical development and mental development is an academic one, especially in the early years.

This kind of co-operation between teacher and therapist is becoming common practice in special care units. It is less common with less severely physically handicapped children, but may still be vitally important if both physical and mental development are to be encouraged.

Adapting learning situations. Having consulted the therapist, a teacher's responsibility does not stop there. She will have to adapt toys and learning experiences so that the child is able to manipulate them. A child who is able to control the movement only of one foot is still able to learn. The lives even of handicapped adults have been transformed by the use of possum typewriters and such ingenious devices. With a young child such highly developed technology may be unnecessary. Toys and puzzles can often be made larger, but not necessarily heavier, so that handicapped children can play with them.

In *Let Me Play*, page 111, we have suggested ways of fastening apparatus firmly to a table top so that clumsy movements will not send it all flying. It is important to position a child so that maximum learning and exploration can take place, and you will find some suggestions in *Let Me Play*, page 61.

Lack of mobility. In some cases a child's weaknesses cannot be readily remedied, so have to be accepted for the time being. Even when a course of treatment has been started (for instance, teaching the child to walk) it may take a long time before it is effective. For the child's sake we cannot afford to wait. An attempt must be made to bypass these weaknesses so that they do not hinder the child's overall development. For example, in the case of a child who is unable to move around by himself, unless special efforts are made on his behalf, this lack of mobility could adversely affect other areas of development. His social development could be held back through lack of opportunity to play with others. He may become even more retarded because it is through seeing and handling toys and experiencing new events that a child learns. Similarly, this may affect his language development and he may have very little opportunity to seek out new experiences or listen to language in an appropriate context.

Even more important, lack of mobility reduces the opportunities for independent action and may lead to a high level of dependency on others.

Wherever possible, each child should be given some means by

which he can explore his environment on his own and decide what he wants to see or whom he wants to talk to. Walking frames are feasible for some children, though only for a minority. But with a lot of ingenuity and some technical help, even children who cannot sit up can be made mobile by the use of boards mounted on castors.

On the other hand in some cases it will not be possible to find a way of enabling a child to get around by himself. If he is unable to seek out experiences himself, then the teacher must devise ways of bringing these experiences to him.

How the teacher can compensate for lack of mobility will depend upon the child's developmental age, and you will find some suggestions in the 'Let Me' books.

Here are a few guidelines.

A responsive environment. An active baby, even when lying in his cot, need not be completely static. By moving his head he can ensure a change of scene, his arm and hand movements will bring him new sensations and new sounds. All these new sensations are vital to his cognitive development. In the case of an immature child who has very little movement, the teacher has to devise a responsive environment to provide these essential changes. For instance, the immature child needs to have a variety of objects to look at, and these should preferably be moving so that he can learn to recognise them in different positions.

Some cerebral palsied children can move very little, and when they can their movements may be uncontrolled. If the child's own minimal movement can be made the agent for changes in the environment this will help the child to realise the relationship between cause and effect. He may also gradually learn to control his own movements in order to bring about the desired effect. Examples of responsive environments can be found in *Let Me Play.*

Learning through imitation. An older child learns a great deal through watching the everyday activities of the people around him, and by joining in these when he is ready. It is important to see that an immobile child does not miss out on these opportunities to learn. It may be possible to prop the child up so that he is in a good position to see everything that is going on. This is not so difficult at home. However, as well as being able to see what people are doing, it is also important to see that the child can also have a hand in these activities. Even in a wheelchair he can be given things to dust, or peas to pod, or cutlery to sort, or pastry to roll out.

Sometimes, however, such activities are not possible in the home and the teacher needs to introduce them into the classroom, so that cakes are made, washing and mending are done in the child's presence, and he is given an opportunity to join in. It is also important that these children are not confined to one room, but are taken out whenever possible to the supermarket, the park and the seaside. Films, slides and pictures are useful, but do not make up for lack of real experience.

A handicapped child should not be debarred from any activity until the teacher has convinced herself that it is impossible for him to join in. Plastic sheeting and protective clothing can minimise the risks in letting handicapped children experience sand and water play, painting and modelling. Where possible the aim should be to devise ways in which the child can do things for himself, rather than having to rely on someone else.

Fine motor co-ordination. In some cases of physical handicap where there is a lack of fine motor co-ordination, or even of an ability to grasp and manipulate objects, efforts must be made to bypass these deficiencies by using whatever motor co-ordination is there. Some children will be able to use a paint brush held in the mouth when they cannot control their hand movements sufficiently to hold the brush in their hand. The aim must be to devise ways of introducing as many normal experiences as possible in the life of the physically handicapped child.

c*

4. Using each child's own interests

You can take a horse to the water, but you cannot make him drink. We may spend a great deal of time devising a teaching game or lesson, only to find that the child will not play it, or that he soon tires of it. Children, as well as adults, have their own individual likes and dislikes which must be respected if we are to teach them effectively. Knowing what a child likes is a positive asset in teaching him and it is well worthwhile spending some time finding out what this is. Some of the children we teach may seem very apathetic at first, and we may be tempted to think that they have no preferences at all. However, a little observation will reveal that most children *do* have something they like more than other things, even if it is only a liking for tearing paper! A record of a child's particular preferences is not only useful for you; it is something to be shared with the parents, the nursery assistant or supply teacher. It is useful to make out a checklist for each child on which you record the child's favourite

(1) *toys and games*;
(2) *person*;
(3) *type of activity*: (*a*) boisterous, (*b*) solitary, (*c*) social;
(4) *specific activities*: (*a*) drawing, (*b*) sandtray, (*c*) water play, (*d*) modelling, (*e*) stories, (*f*) singing or music, etc.;
(5) *position*: (*a*) at table, (*b*) on the floor, (*c*) in the Wendy house, etc.;
(6) *food and drink*.

It is also important to record a child's outstanding dislikes so that these may be avoided. This information will help you in your choice of appropriate activities from the 'Let Me' books.

Remember to keep up to date with your list of favourite activities. Children's preferences sometimes change quite rapidly.

Something to work for. If we want something very much we are usually willing to work for it. This is how progress comes about with children also. If a child wants a toy and it is not quite within reach, he will learn to crawl in order to get it. Similarly, if a child wants a biscuit, he may be encouraged to 'ask for it' before he gets it. At first he may be able to 'ask' only by grunting, but the skilful teacher can gradually step up her demands and eventually get him asking in words. (See *Let Me Speak*, page 58.) If he did not want the biscuit in the first place, however, it is hardly likely that he would make the effort.

If a child is very immature or handicapped, using his preferences may be the only way to start. For instance, a very handicapped boy spent most of his time at school rocking backwards and forwards and moaning. One day the teacher found that he *did* like sitting on her knee and being rocked until his head touched the ground. From time to time she stopped doing this and only re-commenced when he made a sound. Soon he learnt to 'ask' to be rocked by making a grunt and gradually he learnt to say 'more' when he wanted to be rocked. Later he asked by saying 'more' for other things he wanted. Knowing what each child will work for can prove invaluable in our teaching.

Be an opportunist. As well as these fairly stable preferences, teachers need always to be ready to capitalise on more fleeting interests. A child may come to school in a new dress or have just been to a wedding or seen a fire engine. If he is really excited about these new experiences he will find it hard to concentrate on something else. It is a sign of a good teacher that she is flexible enough to make use of these fleeting interests, in order to follow the child's lead. This does not mean that the teacher abandons her initial objective, but uses the child's interests to reach this objective. For instance, the teacher's objective may be to help the child to learn to understand and use three prepositions. She may have carefully prepared a game to help him to learn these, but the child comes to school with his head full of the fire and fire engine he has seen. Instead of focusing the lesson on the apparatus she has prepared, she will then focus it on fire engines and putting out the fire, and introduce the prepositions into this context. The water goes IN the bucket, the fireman climbs UP the ladder and pours the water OVER the fire, etc. It is especially important for the teacher of retarded children to be an opportunist in this way because such interests may be rare occurrences.

5. Using your own interests and talents

As well as making use of the child's own interests and talents, a teacher should also make full use of her own. If you are interested in music or painting or cookery or gardening, bring this into your teaching. Your own genuine enthusiasm will rub off on to the child.

In *Let Me Speak* we have given some examples of how language, for instance, can be encouraged through music or through art. You do not need to be a star performer in order to use your interests in this way. Your enthusiasm is more important than your ability.

Summary

In this chapter we have suggested ways in which the teacher can plan learning situations in order to help individual children. These suggestions include ways in which a teacher may:

(1) use a child's strengths to help overcome some of his weaknesses;

(2) use alternative channels to compensate for irremedial sensory defects;

(3) adapt learning situations for physically handicapped children, and bring vital experiences to them;

(4) use a child's own preferences to encourage further learning;

(5) make full use of her own talents and preferences in order to arouse interest in the child.

5 : Creating Favourable Conditions

This is a practically based chapter which is less concerned with initial planning than with the day-to-day business of helping children to learn, in the classroom, nursery, or in the home.

Special schools vary very much in the provision of space, number of staff and equipment. Whilst it is important to campaign for better conditions, we cannot wait for them: we have to make the best use of what we have got. In this chapter we will suggest ways in which teachers can cut their coat according to the cloth available.

A. PRACTICAL CONSIDERATIONS

When planning a learning situation for a child, or for the children in our care, we have first to make a realistic appraisal of the available amenities. Teaching is concerned with the art of the possible. A little ingenuity will enable the teacher to make the best use of what she has got.

In this chapter we will consider how the teacher can make the best use of the available space, time, personnel and equipment.

Place

When carrying out individual teaching sessions with her pupils, the teacher will aim to provide an attractive and comfortable venue, where she can teach with the minimum of interruptions and in which the child has few distractions and can concentrate on the work in hand.

At this juncture, we can detect hollow laughter and some teachers saying: 'You should come and look at *our* school.'

Others, of course, will be lucky and work in a building which has got individual rooms or annexes which render it comparatively easy to achieve the ideal.

Having had to work with individual children in overcrowded schools ourselves, we would like to hand on the following suggestions.

1. Use of screens

A 'Wendy' house or set of screens are available in most classrooms. It is possible to carry out individual teaching sessions by screening off a corner of the classroom with these. Other children learn to respect this private area and to wait their turn to go into it. Although such an arrangement does not solve the problem of noise, it has been found that children learn to ignore this and to treat this area as their own private world. If screens are unavailable, furniture can sometimes be used to screen off a corner of the classroom (a piano makes an ideal screen), and screens can also be improvised by using old-fashioned clothes-horses draped with curtains, for instance.

2. Use of amenity areas

At home a bedroom can be a good room to use as it is free from distractions. Some of our older schools, while having overcrowded classrooms, have a surprising amount of available space which is lying idle most of the time. We have found that at certain times of the day it is possible to work in cloakroom areas without interruption. If a large board is put over the bath, the bathroom can double up as a teaching room. In one school a large store cupboard was converted for work with individual children. Medical rooms are also sometimes available during part of the school day, though these are not suitable if they have unpleasant connotations for the child.

Wherever you choose for your quiet corner you should bear the following considerations in mind:

(a) *Free from interruptions.* Short, regular, individual sessions are the most effective but these should be free from interruptions.

Other children, and staff, must respect each child's private time.

(*b*) *Few distractions.* Most classrooms in this day and age are very stimulating and colourful. For some children they are almost too stimulating and distracting. If we want a child to concentrate on a particular teaching game, we should remove all other distractions. It may be enough to cover these up with a cloth, *before* the child comes into the area. The teaching material should then be made as attractive as possible, but be the only thing to attract the child.

(*c*) *Comfort.* If we are going to use odd areas of the school for our teaching, we will have to ensure that they are comfortable for the child; that he is seated comfortably and that the working space is at the right height. It is also important to see that the area is well lit and heated and that it is not airless.

(*d*) *Introduce the teaching area.* A child's first impressions often colour his whole attitude to learning. If he has been frightened or put off at his first session, it will be difficult to make him feel at home at a later stage. Time taken to introduce each child to his new 'home' is time well spent. Initially, it is important that he should connect it with something he likes very much; perhaps a favourite toy or activity. Do not be in too much of a hurry to begin. Encourage each child to look forward to his 'turn' as something special, and terminate the session if the child shows any sign of stress.

(*e*) *Avoid chopping and changing.* It is important, for the child's sake, to try to avoid continually chopping and changing. Children are creatures of habit and we can make use of this. Try, if possible, to ensure that each child's daily session is always held in the same place. If you have to change it, think carefully about each individual child. Some children can tolerate change more easily than others.

Time

One argument against individual teaching sessions is lack of time. However, it must be remembered that it is not the *length* of time available that matters, but how that time is used. The well planned use of five minutes a day is often of greater value than irregular periods of half an hour. A teacher needs to work out her priorities very carefully, and to decide how much time she can give to each child in a one-to-one situation.

The following guidelines will help her to do this:

(a) *The child needs to be alert.* Some children work best in the morning, others seem to need a longer period to adjust them-selves to the school situation, and work best in the afternoon. The teacher needs to note these individual differences and try to plan so that each child has his teaching session when he is most alert.

(b) *The teacher needs to be alert.* Keep yourself in mind when planning sessions. Choose a time when you are feeling alert! Friday afternoon may not be the best time for any of the sessions. Your keenness will often help a child to overcome his initial apathy.

(c) *Establish a routine.* Try to establish a routine so that each child knows when to expect his session with you. Retarded children may find it hard to express their disappointment at not getting what they expected. This does not mean that they do not feel it.

(d) *Keep the sessions short.* You need to do this if you are to get around all your pupils. We have already pointed out that short sessions at regular intervals are more effective than longer, more sporadic sessions. Another good rule is: always stop BEFORE the child wants to. If you drag the lesson on and finish on a negative note, the child will be less keen to come to the session next time. If the child finishes the session while he is still interested, he will be all the more eager for the next instalment!

(e) *Make use of caretaking time.* It is not always easy to fit in regular teaching sessions for each child during a busy school day. Especially when very young or handicapped children are concerned, a great deal of time is taken up in caretaking activities, such as toileting, feeding, etc. This is also true at home.

In feeding, toileting and dressing you will need to give each child some individual attention. This time need not be wasted. It can present an ideal opportunity for developing functional language, for instance. If the teacher can also introduce an element of choice into these situations, this will help to encourage the child to speak.

Personnel

One of the biggest difficulties in the way of helping each individual child is the lack of trained personnel. However, there are often people available who might be able to help. Many classrooms have ancillary staff; it is quite common for older school children to come in one day a week to help; or parents may come in to help in the classroom. Full use of extra help can only be made by the teacher who has planned out a precise teaching scheme for each child. After having got this started, she can often hand over to someone else—but only if she has taken the time and trouble to tell them exactly what to do, to let them watch her at work, and also to watch them herself for a session or two.

Similarly, parents can often find neighbours, grandparents and friends willing and able to work with their children, as long as they know exactly what to do. Some people will develop unexpected talents in this direction. It is often wise to involve other members of the family in this way, for a short period every day. Later chapters will suggest ways of assessing progress and using recording procedures to help to ensure consistency of methods between different people.

Equipment

Toys and equipment seem to get more expensive and less worth the money every year, and, at the same time, money for requisitions is being cut. Fortunately, good can come even from this unsatisfactory situation. The best equipment is not always the most expensive. Most of the toys used in *Let Me Speak* or *Let Me Play* can be made from junk, or made cheaply by a handyman (or woman) with a few simple tools.

The following points should prove a useful guide to buying or making equipment:

1. Durability

Retarded children will often be bigger and stronger and, possibly, more clumsy than other children by the time they are ready to play with toys. When buying equipment it is important to ask the question 'Will it stand up to wear and tear?'

It is especially important in the case of the larger items of equipment, such as slides and see-saws. These may be made to bear the weight of small children, but will not stand up to the strain imposed by mentally immature but physically well-developed older children.

Similarly, pedal-cars and tricycles will need to be very sturdy and big enough for the children who are going to use them. Of course, not all mentally handicapped children are physically well developed. In some cases growth is stunted and smaller equipment will be required. However, it is easier to adapt a piece of equipment which is too large than one that is too small. For instance, pedal-cars can be adapted by screwing blocks on to the pedals for the smaller children. It is important to check equipment for size, as otherwise it may prove too difficult to work with, or may be very uncomfortable for the child.

Many smaller toys, especially plastic ones, are not stable enough for a clumsy child to use: they require a great deal of manual dexterity to prevent them from overturning or flying off the table, and are also easily broken. Wooden toys are usually sturdier and can also be clamped down to a table if necessary, or screwed on to a bench.

2. *Safety*

Many toys are tested for safety, and this is true of most play-things made in this country. However, toys from abroad and cheap toys sometimes fail to come up to safety standards. The points to check are:

    (*a*) *Paint.* This can be toxic if it contains lead. Handicapped children often suck their toys, as most small children do, but since they continue to do this over long periods it is doubly important to make sure that the paint is not toxic.

    (*b*) *Detachable parts.* It is especially important to check soft toys for detachable parts. Teddy bears' eyes are sometimes fastened on with spiky lengths of wire, as also are the legs and arms. These parts need to be checked, and it may be necessary to remove them, and re-assemble the toy with strong linen thread instead of wire.

3. *Versatility*

Initially, when you are laying out money for basic equipment, the best toys to buy will be those which are most versatile. Many 'educational' toys, whilst they may be useful for teaching one specific skill, are soon expendable. If a child continues to play with them over and over again in the same way, he will not be learning anything new.

An example of a reasonably versatile toy might be a simple ring-stack: for with this toy, a child can learn to match colours, name them, distinguish shapes and become more skilful with his hands. However, once he is able to stack the pieces easily and name the colours and shapes, he will learn very little by playing with this toy. (In *Let Me Play*, we have described a series of ring-stacks which are increasingly difficult and so extend the child's skill, page 120.) Other toys are much more versatile. A good example is a ball, this can be used for rolling or for simple catching, throwing, hitting a target, or in playing cricket or tennis or football!

As you see, the simpler toys are, the more versatile is their use. In *Let Me Speak* and *Let Me Play*, we have used a relatively small number of toys, but each toy can be used in a variety of ways, to help manual dexterity, colour and shape recognition, comprehension and production of single words, putting two words together and memory games. A child can continue to play with a versatile toy without being bored when he is learning something new every time.

Parents would be well advised to visit their local Toy Library. In this way they can try out different toys and often get expert advice.

4. Specifically graded toys

As well as having a good stock of versatile toys which can be used in many different ways, a teacher will often require a series of toys specifically geared to an individual child's needs. It is seldom possible to buy toys which exactly fit the bill, for a handicapped child will often need a finely graded series of toys to help increase his skill one step at a time. Also, each child's specific requirements may be different from another's, and they will each need different toys.

We have used a graded series of form-boards, not only to increase manual dexterity and shape recognition, but also in building up an effective vocabulary.

Although such apparatus is not on the market, it is not too difficult to make.

It is important, however, to make sure that you have a good stock of basic materials to hand, as well as a few essential tools.

We have found that, in addition to the usual stock of pictures, card, paper·and paint and crayons, the following materials are the most useful: off-cuts of wood, lengths of dowelling of varying thicknesses, plywood and hardboard.

A collection of junk materials is also invaluable for making apparatus: for instance, cotton reels, boxes, cream cartons, bottle-tops, corks, squeezy bottles, polystyrene packing, pipe-cleaners, scraps of material, shells, and so on.

Essential tools include scissors, a sharp knife, drills, a brace and bits, screw-driver, hammer, tenon saw and fretsaw, and clamps, as well as woodworkers' adhesive.

5. Simplicity and imagination

The toy shops are full of increasingly complicated and realistic toys: dolls which walk and talk, models which are exact replicas of real planes, etc. But these sophisticated toys leave very little to the imagination, and may accordingly be unsatisfying to the child. Expensive dolls with every detail correct are often eventually left on one side in favour of a shapeless 'teddy' who has lost his eyes and is rather grubby. With the simpler toy the child has to add the details himself, he must *imagine* that the teddy is dressed for a party or is feeling sad or is saying, 'Bye-bye!' Sometimes he can pretend his teddy is a policeman or a teacher, another time he may pretend it is a baby. In *Let Me Speak* we have described the importance in child development of this ability to pretend, and how it can be fostered (page 64). One way of helping to foster the imagination is by giving the child simple toys which lend themselves to imaginative play, and then showing the child different ways of playing with them. This is very important in language development. Simple rag dolls and cardboard boxes of different sizes, simple shapes on wheels and containers of all kinds can be used in this way.

Household objects. Nor do all toys have to come from toy shops. Some household objects provide simple and effective playthings. In *Let Me Play* we have described the use of screw-top jars, wooden spoons and coffee tins as playthings.

As we have already mentioned, junk material can also be used most effectively. For instance, skittles can be made from squeezy bottles.

6. Intrinsically interesting toys

It is important to avoid making play into a lesson. A child will learn much more from a game if he is playing because HE wants to, rather than because he has been coaxed into the situation. In choosing toys it is important to keep this in mind. Toys are likely to attract children if *something happens* when they play with them. The flashing clown described in *Let Me Play* (page 121) is a good example of such a toy. Even an immature child will play with this toy of his own accord in order to see the eyes flash and hear the 'bleeper'. Other examples of 'cause and effect' toys are listed in *Let Me Play*, page 42.

Summary

To sum up, the best apparatus or toy is:

(1) durable;
(2) safe;
(3) versatile;
(4) specifically graded;
(5) simple;
(6) intrinsically interesting.

6 : Teaching Skills

INTRODUCTION

One of the hallmarks of a good teacher is her ability to obtain and retain a child's interest in a teaching game, so that the child does not 'go off' the activity, but eagerly participates in his own learning.

Second, a teacher needs to be able to organise such a game so as to ensure that progressive learning is taking place and that it does not develop into a static activity. The teacher needs also to convey to the child not only an awareness of the nature of the task, but also the satisfaction of knowing he is doing it well.

These are just some of the skills which teachers require. And although teaching skills develop through practice, they are not dependent upon practice alone.

In this chapter, by outlining certain fundamental principles which apply to most teaching situations we shall suggest ways in which teachers can begin to acquire these skills. The careful application of these principles should enhance the effectiveness of any teacher, even the most experienced one.

The first part of the chapter will deal with ways of getting a child's attention and retaining his interest, then with ways of decreasing the occurrence of disruptive and inappropriate behaviour patterns.

In the second part of the chapter, we shall discuss the problem of lack of co-operation which may arise when the child is unclear as to what is expected of him. We shall suggest ways of getting the message across to children whose knowledge of the spoken word may be either very rudimentary or completely absent.

The third part of the chapter is concerned with grading the demands we make upon children, so that they progress a step at a time without undue stress.

Lastly, we shall suggest ways of giving feedback to the child so that he knows exactly what he is expected to do.

GETTING THE CHILD'S ATTENTION AND RETAINING HIS INTEREST

Although many mentally retarded children develop an interest in toys and are fairly easily encouraged to extend their play, others may not play at all and are very seriously lacking in concentration. Some children may be overactive so that they do not stop long enough with any one game to learn from it; others are not very sociable and may react badly to being 'shown' what to do; and others still may be very destructive.

We have already suggested the importance of choosing your time and place with each child (see page 75). In this section we shall outline other guidelines concerned with getting a child's attention and retaining his interest.

1. Setting the scene

As every mother knows, there are ways of getting a child's attention and interest even in the most adverse circumstances. Parents often have to get children to take medicine, stay in bed, or do other things they are unwilling to do, and in developing their own strategies they have probably been guided by the principles we are about to describe.

(a) *The teacher's attitude*. Teachers sometimes reject learning games out of hand, saying 'The children would be bored doing that'. What they really mean is that *they* would be bored, and there is no surer way of boring children than being bored yourself. The teacher's attitude is probably one of the most important elements in education. A teacher needs to summon up fresh enthusiasm each time a game is played, no matter how simple it seems to her. A reluctant child should not be coaxed to play a new game. Rather he should be lured into wanting to play it. It often helps if the teacher gets down on the floor and starts playing herself; at first making no attempt to attract the child, but showing a great deal of interest and enthusiasm in playing the game. This ruse may have to be repeated several times, until eventually the child himself makes the first move to join in. Our observations of children throughout the day will be proof positive of the practical instances of this principle. When adults are ignoring the children and are engaged in work of their own, the children will often leave their childish pursuits and try to join in—in using the 'phone, typing on your typewriter—and this in spite of the fact that you have given them no encouragement.

(b) *Use of special toys.* A child's individual session should be dressed up so that it is a treat which he looks forward to. At first, it is best to use special toys for these sessions as they will add to the element of anticipation. A child's attention can often be increased if an element of mystery is introduced to increase his anticipation, for instance the toys may appear from the depths of a bag or box.

(c) *Use of variety.* Perhaps one of the greatest disservices to children is to bore them. One way of preventing boredom is by the use of variety. In the 'Let Me' books, we have shown how several different games can be played to teach the same thing. Another way of introducing variety is to add new elements to the same game. Of course, some children do like to repeat a familiar game over and over again. This is fair enough, so long as the teacher makes sure that it does not go too far, and end up in stereotyped behaviour which is not teaching the child anything new. Even with these children it is important to introduce variety, perhaps only a little at a time to start with. A few children react very badly to a change of routine and the teacher will need all her art to arrive at the right mixture of 'sameness' and 'change'.

2. Arousing and maintaining interests

It is said that work is something we do for a reward, and play is an activity which is carried out for its own sake. Our aims should always be to make the game so intrinsically interesting that the child will play it because he wants to and not for any external reward or praise. In order to achieve this aim we should keep the following points in mind:

(a) *Children usually like to do something they can do well.* It is important to plan games which ensure that the child does not fail. For instance, we have described a fetching game in *Let Me Speak* (page 82) which is aimed at teaching a child to understand single words. At first only one toy is used, so that when the teacher asks for a 'doll' there is only a doll available, and the child cannot fail to bring the correct object. The same game will then be played with another toy on its own. Now when the teacher asks for a 'car' the child cannot fail to find the right object because he has no choice. Only after he has got the hang of this game do you put the two toys on the floor. Now, when the teacher asks for a 'doll', there is a possibility of failure to bring the right object. The child might bring a 'car'. Even this should be avoided as much as possible and, at first, the teacher may have to point to the object as well as asking for it. Eventually the child will have learnt to understand these two words and bring the right object without any extra help. This gives the child plenty of opportunities to experience success.

(b) *Something happens when you play.* A very young child learns to turn on the electric light, and he will go on doing this without any outside encouragement! He will be intrigued by the consequence of his action, i.e. the light coming on. It is possible to use this principle to get him playing other, more desirable, games. In the flashing clown game (*Let Me Play*, page 121) a child learns to stack rings because this is how he can make lights come on. This game was based on a child's natural interest in lights. Most children are also naturally interested in poking things into holes and finding out what happens. Posting games, based on this intrinsic interest, will often hold a child's attention (see *Let Me Speak*, page 81).

(c) *Giving extra help and combating boredom.* A child may lose interest in a game if it is a little too difficult and he finds it frustrating. He may enjoy playing the game if given a little extra help. Even if the child is only watching the game when the teacher is showing him how to do it, she should not give up too soon; the day will come when he will do it for himself. If he can play the game and is getting bored, some new element should be added. At first he will need a great deal of encouragement.

(d) *Making it more interesting.* Some mentally handicapped children have to be taught how to play initially. They may not have any idea of what to do and, however carefully the game is chosen, they will not find it reinforcing.

Until they have started to play they will not get any pleasure from their toys, nor learn from them. At this stage you do not want to wait until the child starts to play of his own accord. He may not do this for a long time, and in the meanwhile he is losing out on the experience he could get through play. You have to find something which will make the game more interesting. The first step is to find out something which the child likes: this may be ice-cream, a biscuit, or a small sweet. Use tiny portions as a reward. (However, it does not need to be food and we have already described using a child's fascination with lights.) For instance, we might want to get a child turning the pages of a book and looking at the pictures. Hold his hand and turn a page with him and *immediately* it is turned, pop a tiny spoonful of ice-cream into his mouth. Do this several times until he has got the idea and starts to turn the pages on his own. Give him the reward *every* time at first, and as you give it to him, praise him as well. When he is doing this well on his own you need not reward him every time. Let him look at two pictures before getting a reward and then three, until gradually he will be able to look at every page and get his reward only when he has finished the book! Do not forget to encourage him with praise. Eventually, the child will look at the pictures because of the enjoyment it gives him and he will no longer need the ice-cream. Do not over-use this type of reward. Some children will not need it at all; the praise will be enough reward. Or give them a little clap when they do well. Later you will not need to clap them every time, but only occasionally. Whatever reward you use the principle is still the same. Start off by using it every time, then *gradually* use it less and less so that he has to do more before getting it.

(e) *Stop while you have his attention.* One difficult principle to apply in practice is to stop a game while you still have the child's attention and co-operation. If you go on too long you run the risk of ending the session on a negative note. The child may have lost interest or wandered off. This may have a deleterious effect on future sessions. The child begins to associate the game with boredom and frustration. If, however, you finish the game when he is still wanting it to continue, you will build up a mood of pleasurable anticipation and it will become increasingly easy to gain his co-operation.

Dealing with inappropriate behaviour
When, in spite of careful planning, a child continues to behave inappropriately, for instance tearing pictures, throwing books on the floor, or overturning the table, the teacher needs to take careful stock of the situation.

First, observe the child's behaviour and *your* behaviour. It is possible that your own actions are inadvertently maintaining the child's disruptive behaviour. Let us consider what a teacher might do when a child is misbehaving. One thing she might do is try and coax him back into the game. Or she might get very cross and shout at him, or even give him a smack. Alternatively, she might take hold of his hand and sit him firmly back into the chair and start again. All these ways of coping are fine, *so long as they work*! If they don't work, it is well worth while to sit down and consider why. Let us look at these methods of control, one at a time.

1. Coaxing
Why is coaxing often ineffective? When a teacher is coaxing a

child, she tends to give him all her attention, and exert her charm so long as he is *not* doing whatever she requires. As soon as the child complies with her wishes, she often eases off and gives him less attention. Think about this. A child who is not eating his cabbage gets a lot of attention, teachers may even encourage him by reciting rhymes, 'One for the pussy cat—' and so on. As soon as he starts to eat it up on his own, the teacher heaves a sigh of relief and lets him get on with it! Often, this only leads to more refusal, because the child loves the extra attention and learns that the way to get it is by 'playing up'. In fact the teacher is not making him *less* naughty, but encouraging him to be naughtier.

2. Getting cross and shouting

Raising your voice in order to control behaviour works with some children. It should be used sparingly, however. If you are always raising your voice the child will learn to ignore this warning. With some children, raising your voice does not work at all. They seem to enjoy being shouted at. At least their behaviour is receiving some immediate attention. Getting a grown-up to raise his voice may become a game in its own right.

3. Physical control

Picking the child up bodily and sitting him down to play the game is called physical control. Why is this often ineffective? Well, some children enjoy physical contact, they like rough and tumble games when they are being pulled about and moved. They may not be old enough to realise that this is 'not a game'. Every time they get up from the chair the teacher puts them back again; if they tip the table over the teacher puts it back. Some children really seem to enjoy this situation; *they* are in control, not the teacher. The trouble about this kind of disruptive behaviour is that it is catching!

4. Indiscriminate praise

All through this book we have stressed the importance of being positive and not being niggardly with your praise. This does not mean you should praise the child whatever he does. Only praise the kind of behaviour you want and be sure you time your praise carefully. One little boy we knew indulged in inappropriate behaviour from time to time. He would suddenly tip all the crayons on the floor. His mother, wisely, insisted on him picking them all up and putting them back in the tin. When he had done this she hugged him and praised him. However, she rather overdid the praise. No sooner had he been praised than he tipped the crayons out again to get some more of the same!

5. Pack up before a child 'spoils the game'
Try never to let a child spoil a teaching game. Immediately he starts to do this, remove the toys and any rewards you are using and walk away. In some cases, you may be able to resume the game in a very short time when you see the child has sat down and is ready to play it properly. If he 'plays up' again, the best thing is to terminate that session for the day. Remember, actions speak louder than words and you do not need to say anything, neither praise nor blame. The child will soon learn his lesson and he will learn it all the sooner if you are quite impassive about this.

Whatever your method of control, the golden rule is to ask 'does it work?' By that we mean, is the child's behaviour gradually improving or not? If your method does *not* work, you may be interested in the following suggestions. You may not think *they* will work either, but do not dismiss them without giving them a fair trial. Whatever method you use, it is important to be consistent and to give the method time to work.

Here then is a summary of some suggestions which we have found most effective in getting and maintaining a child's interest.

1. Make the teaching game worthwhile
Your teaching game has to be more attractive than 'bad' behaviour. Make sure that it is fun and it is rewarding to the child. Make sure he gets plenty of attention and praise when he

is doing the 'right' thing. Make sure that the game is not too difficult and do not expect him to play it too long.

2. Never give extra attention to bad behaviour
Whenever possible bad behaviour should not result in any extra attention. We suggest that such behaviour, by and large, should be ignored. We know that some actions, like kicking another child, cannot be ignored completely. We may have to take some action. In this case, the important thing to remember is to do what we must, quite *impersonally*. Try to treat the child as if he were a piece of furniture. Avoid eye contact or praise or blame.

3. Go out of your way to give extra attention to good behaviour
If a child is often indulging in inappropriate behaviour, it is important to be on the alert to catch him when he is behaving well. Make a fuss of him and reward him for this; even if he is only sitting still.

4. Avoid confrontation with the child
If a child is spoiling the game or acting inappropriately, simply pack up the session for the time being.

SHOWING THE CHILD WHAT IS EXPECTED OF HIM

We sometimes forget that, although it is obvious to us how a teaching game should be played, or how a special toy should be used, this may be a complete mystery to the child we are dealing with.

Years of experience have taught us that balls are for throwing and doll's teasets are not. Many handicapped children, like all babies, have not discovered this yet. Some of the games outlined in the 'Let Me' books depend upon much more subtle conventions as to how they can profitably be played.

The teacher is frequently confronted with a child who is failing to do what is expected of him. She may assume that she has chosen a task which is too difficult and, if this is the case, she will have to backtrack to something simpler.

However, it is not always safe to assume that the task is too difficult. A child sometimes fails because he simply does not understand what he is expected to do.

It is vitally important that you get your message across, especially when you are introducing a new activity.

There are several different ways of making clear to a child what you are expecting him to do. The method you use will largely depend upon the maturity of the child.

We shall now outline some of the methods we can use to get our message across.

Showing a child what to do

Luckily, a child does not have to understand what we say before he can learn from us. Long before a child can understand the spoken word, he will start to try to copy our actions and learn by imitation. And even when he is beginning to understand the spoken word, he will often learn more from an object lesson.

Modelling

Showing a child what to do by doing it in front of him is called modelling. We can provide good models or bad, and here are some guidelines to good modelling:

(a) *It must be clear, and uncluttered.* Model an action, e.g. putting a piece into a form-board, very deliberately, so that every detail of the action is clear: picking the piece up, turning it round the right way, making sure it goes right in, and so on. It is especially important to give clear models when helping the child to learn language: i.e. to say the words naturally but deliberately, so that they can be distinguished from other, similar words.

(b) *It must be repeated several times.* A child is not likely to copy our model when he has seen it only once. Be content for him to watch you several times before expecting him to imitate.

(c) *Do not give up too soon.* Many handicapped children will not immediately copy our model, even after watching us several times. However, do not give up too soon. We have found, in practice, that imitation is often delayed. For instance, one day you may not be able to get the child to wave 'Bye-bye' however hard you try: then perhaps the next day he will suddenly do it. You have to give the child time to rehearse the action in his own mind. This is a very important maxim to remember when we are introducing language, otherwise we may be tempted to give up the language game at the most crucial moment.

(d) *Model at the right level.* It is impossible for anyone to imitate a series of actions which go far beyond their level of experience. A child may fail to pick up our model because it is either at the wrong level, or too complex for him.

(e) *Get the child's attention.* Do not waste too much time demonstrating when the child is not attending to you but is looking elsewhere. When he is looking at you, that is the time to do the modelling.

Using other children as models. It is sometimes very effective to get another child to model a game, instead of an adult. Both children can learn from this situation. As well as interacting, the other child has an opportunity to consolidate and organise his own learning.

Parents will find that older siblings form a happier relationship with the handicapped child if they have a specific role to play. Often you can involve them in the teaching as models for the handicapped child.

In the classroom ancillary helpers, as well as other children, can also be used to 'model' games.

However, whoever is doing or organising the modelling needs to be made aware of the guidelines we have already noted.

Telling the child what to do. This is the most commonly used method for getting the message across to children, but probably the least appropriate where young handicapped children are concerned. While including this method we would suggest that other methods are usually preferable.

D

We would not dream of giving young mental handicapped children written instructions, knowing that they would be incapable of reading them and understanding them. However, we do give them verbal instructions and it is worth considering whether they are able to understand and follow these. In order to get the message across, you must:

(a) *Use only words he understands.* If a child is only just learning to label toys and to understand you when you ask for a doll, or a ball, he will not yet understand the word 'not'; if you ask for a ball and he brings you the doll, you will only muddle him if you say, 'That's *not* a ball'. 'Ball' will be the only word he understands and he will go on thinking that that is the name of the doll.

(b) *Keep your instructions short and consistent.* Sometimes children need time to think about what you have told them to do. After giving an instruction, wait a while before repeating it. If you talk too much, this will only confuse the child; he will have to try to concentrate on two things at once, i.e. on what you are saying and on what he has to do.

(c) *A child may not understand the spoken word on its own.* In order to help him, match your words with appropriate actions. While saying: 'Put the picture in the box', demonstrate what you mean. Or, if he does not respond when you tell him to 'Find the blue one', then help him by pointing to it. Gradually give less and less help until he can follow the verbal instructions without any further cues.

Another way of showing a child what we expect him to do is by prompting him. We will expand the use of prompts later on in the chapter.

GRADING OUR DEMANDS

So far, our attention has been directed towards showing a child what we want him to do. We have discussed a number of different ways of doing this, all with the same objective; the child is left in no doubt as to what is expected of him.

However, it is not sufficient for the child to get a clear idea of what we expect unless he is also able to fulfil our expectations. Nor should the demands we make be static, we have constantly to make fresh demands on the child.

We have to be very careful about the sort of demands we make or we are in for trouble. Normal children can take a bit of a leap in their learning, but a handicapped child can often learn only one step at a time.

However, in order to grade our demands in this way, we need to have analysed the task in the first place.

Task Analysis. Having decided what you want a child to learn, bearing in mind his present capabilities, the next thing is to break the action down into small steps. Even the simplest task involves a number of steps.

For instance, you might have decided to teach a child to put on his jacket. We do this automatically every day. But try standing in front of a mirror and slowly putting on your own jacket. Note down everything you did in order, like this:

(1) pick up jacket by the neck;
(2) turn the jacket round so that the sleeves are in the right position;
(3) hold the lapel with left hand;
(4) push right arm through right sleeve;
(5) let go with left hand;
(6) put left arm behind back;
(7) feel around for armhole;
(8) push left hand into armhole;
(9) wriggle jacket on to shoulders;
(10) adjust collar with both hands;
(11) adjust opening to meet.

That is quite a tall order, even without doing up the buttons! You may find that an even finer analysis is needed and that eleven stages are not enough; for instance step 4 could be broken down into three stages: putting arm in, pushing it through and getting it out.

Presented with the whole task at once, a child will almost certainly experience failure, and this is what we want to avoid.

However, we can grade our demands in either of the following ways:

A. Forward chaining

In forward chaining a child learns to do the task one step at a time, and in the order in which it is normally carried out. That is, he learns to pick up the jacket first, then to turn the jacket round, and so on.

If each step is learnt in isolation, the exercise may appear rather pointless. The child will have no idea what 'picking up a jacket' is leading to. He will only get the idea when he has mastered all the steps and has the satisfaction of completing the task and being ready to go out.

However, it is not necessary to teach each stage out of context. Teachers will often let the child start the task by picking up the jacket and then they will do the rest of the task for the child, in order that he gets the idea of the complete process.

Very independent children, once having started the proceedings, will be reluctant to hand over to the adult. In this case, an alternative method of teaching would probably work better:

B. Backward chaining

In backward chaining, the child learns the sequence of steps in reverse order. The teacher almost completes the task but leaves the child to do the last step. For instance, when you are teaching him to put on his jacket, you do it all for him except the last action—i.e. leave him to adjust the openings to meet. Once he has mastered this step you leave two actions for him to complete and so on until he can do it all by himself. This has advantages. In this kind of task, (a) the child always has the satisfaction of completing the task and so feeling he has done it;

(*b*) the child always finishes up with something he can do well and not with a newly learnt skill; and (*c*) the child has plenty of opportunity to learn the next step, as you will have demonstrated it for him every time.

Skills Analysis. As we discussed in Section 1, it is important before embarking on teaching any task to analyse it in terms of the basic skills involved (see page 39).

In the task of putting on his jacket, a child needs to have hand-eye co-ordination, manual dexterity, and the complementary use of both hands. He needs to have a body awareness and to be able to position objects in relation to his own body, and so on.

It is important to know what skills are required for any given task. Until the child has developed these skills, he will be unable to put them together in sequence. So as well as practicing the stages involved in the task itself give the child practice at the skills. Many of the basic skills are needed for a great many other tasks. For instance, threading beads also requires hand-eye co-ordination, manual dexterity and the complementary use of both hands.

When teaching basic skills the keyword is variety. Do not use a single game to help a child learn to use both his hands, for instance. The child will find it much more interesting if you play a variety of games. We are aiming at the flexible use of these skills, rather than training one isolated set of behaviours. If a child is accustomed to using his newly found skills in a variety of ways, he will learn to generalise his skill much better.

Analysing a task into its component parts is another way of grading your demands on the child. You will be teaching him one skill at a time, and when he has mastered the component skills he will be ready to combine them in a more difficult task.

Prompting
Another way of grading our demands on a child is by giving the child some extra help or prompt until he is ready to complete the task on his own.

This is a very useful aid to teaching and we will outline a variety of prompts which most teachers will have used at one time or another. For instance, when a child is having difficulty a teacher will often point to the correct piece in a jigsaw, guide his hand, or tell him which to pick.

In this part of the chapter we shall spell out the systematic use of a variety of prompts, their advantages and disadvantages, and how they can be gradually discontinued.

1. Physical prompts

Physical prompts are often used for very young babies. For instance, a mother shows a baby how to wave 'bye-bye' by taking his arm and waving it for him. This kind of prompt is also useful for older children who are passive, or failing to explore the toys in their environment.

These physical prompts should be considered as a temporary measure only. The ultimate aim is to get the child acting on his own. The abandonment of prompts may be a very real problem; the child may learn to rely on prompts, so that once they are removed he will continue to flounder.

This can be largely avoided if prompts are carefully faded out in the following way. The example we have taken is prompting a child to feed himself. These are the stages:

Fading

(a) The parents or teacher prompts the child throughout the whole action sequence, i.e. she puts her hand over his and picks up the spoon, moves it to the plate, shovels the food in, moves the spoon and hand to his mouth, and tips the food in. All the child has to do on his own, is eat the food!

(b) The parent or teacher prompts the child as before, but, if he seems to be getting some control of his actions, she gently releases her hand just before the spoon reaches his mouth and leaves him to do the last little bit on his own.

(c) Now the parent or teacher leaves go of the child's hand when the spoon still has some inches to go on its journey to the mouth.

You will now have got the idea! At each stage the child has a little more of the action to do on his own. Also at each stage, it is he who always completes the action and is rewarded for doing so—in this case by having something to eat! (see backward chaining).

The teacher must gauge how quickly such physical prompts can be faded out. This will depend upon the child. You can easily see when you have faded out the prompts too soon—the food will be spilled!

The main *advantages* of physical prompts are:

(a) They give the child a clear idea of what is expected of him;
(b) they enable the child to experience the movements involved in the task when he is still physically unable to carry them out on his own;
(c) physical prompts are most useful to overcome specific skills which the child lacks.

The main disadvantage of physical prompts is:
they can lead to excessive dependence on the adult. This can be avoided if the prompts are faded out as soon as they are no longer needed.

2. Gestural prompts

Pointing is one kind of gestural prompt, but there are many more. For instance, we may want a child to pick out a picture of a ball from an array of pictures. As well as saying 'ball' we might describe a circle with our hands. Sometimes we use this kind of prompt without being aware that we are doing so. Nodding our head in the right direction, or even looking pointedly at the right choice, are both examples of gestural prompts. It is important to be aware of this—and to check up if the child has really learnt to do without them.

These prompts are important to language learning. Even before a child understands or uses words, he may understand gestures. In early language learning, gestures should be paired with words (see *Let Me Speak*, page 71). However, it is important that these gestures should be consistent. For instance, when we are teaching the child the use of the word 'EAT', we pretend to eat. Indeed, where a child's language is unusually delayed, a structural system of gesture or sign language, such as the Paget-Gorman system, linked with the spoken word often helps the child to learn to speak. As with other prompts, gestural prompts should be gradually faded out if the child really is to learn the skill for himself.

Advantages of gestural prompts
- (*a*) Gestural prompts leave a child freer than physical prompts. Although we are guiding him towards the correct action, the choice is still his.
- (*b*) There is nothing unusual in the use of simple gestural prompts. They can be used at any time without loss of dignity on either side.

Disadvantage. Unless everyone is consistent in the gestures they use, the message will not be clear to the child. Teachers and parents should agree on the gestures to be used.

3. Verbal prompts
The most commonly used prompts in teaching are verbal ones, such as 'Put the red brick in the box'. These should be monitored very carefully, bearing in mind what it is we are trying to teach.

Here are some points to note:

(*a*) *Avoid making the verbal prompts too complicated or long.* Much of learning consists of making a choice—for instance, between the red brick or the blue one. There is no need to elaborate by saying 'Pick up the red brick and put it on the stack', when all the information the child needs is contained in the one word 'red'.

(*b*) *Match your verbal prompt to the child's level of understanding.* In the previous example, if the child understands only single words, you are making it harder rather than easier for him by talking in sentences.

(c) *Do not confuse a child by giving inconsistent prompts.* Decide what you want the child to do and prompt him on *this* only. Do not change your prompt in mid-stream. For instance, you may want the child to learn to sit down to drink his milk. You start by saying 'Sit down', then change to 'Don't stand there': 'There's the chair'. This may only confuse the child.

(d) *Use positive rather than negative prompts.* The word *not* is one that takes a long time to understand. If the child makes the wrong choice and gives you a blue brick instead of a red one, it is preferable to shake your head or say 'NO', and then repeat the word RED. If you say '*Not* the blue one', he is likely to get confused and think you do want the blue one.

(e) *Tone of voice is important.* Saying 'fine' or 'yes' is another kind of verbal prompt which lets the child know when he is right. Similarly, '*no*' lets him know when he is wrong. Your tone of voice, no less than your actual words, is important here.

Fading. As with other prompts, verbal prompts should be reduced to the minimum and gradually faded out or used intermittently, in order to get the child able to work or play on his own.

Advantages of verbal prompts
- (a) Properly used verbal prompts indicate clearly what you intend the child to do.
- (b) Verbal prompts help children to link actions with words and later to direct their own actions.
- (c) A child is still free to act independently and to exercise some choice. Thus when you say 'Get the blue one' there may be several blue objects. The child can choose from these and still be right. This distinguishes verbal prompts from physical or gestural prompts.

D*

Disadvantages of verbal prompts

(*a*) We are so used to *telling* people what to do that we are in danger of overdoing it. Such prompts are far more telling if used sparingly.

(*b*) The language comprehension of many handicapped children is often very rudimentary. In this case verbal prompts can be inappropriate.

(*c*) Some children learn to ignore verbal commands if they are bombarded with these throughout the day.

4. Situational prompts

Prompts can be provided by the teaching situation itself, and the way in which toys and apparatus are presented. For instance, we have described in *Let Me Speak* a way of increasing a child's understanding of single words by getting him to bring single objects to his teacher. At first, only one word is introduced and the teacher says 'Give me ball'. In order to prompt the child to make a correct response, he is given no choice. The ball is the only toy available and it is in a prominent position. This prompt is gradually faded out, when he has got the idea of bringing the ball. Two objects are now placed in a prominent position side by side. The teacher asks again, 'Give me ball', and this time there is a choice. If the child fails to bring the ball, then the teacher must backtrack. She will still use two objects, but put the ball slightly nearer the child than the other toy.

Once he has learnt to choose the ball from an array of two, then a third toy is introduced, and so on.

Advantages of situational prompts

(*a*) Situational prompts leave the child relatively free to act independently.

(*b*) By this means, you can increase the child's probability of success.

Disadvantage. Situational prompts require a great deal of planning and organisation on the part the teacher.

Feedback

When a child fails in a task, we have to ask ourselves why? It is not necessarily because he cannot do it.

Frequently a child will fail because he is not quite sure what he is supposed to do. He looks to us for feedback: that is to confirm that he has done the right thing. There are many different ways of doing this: we may say 'good', or give him a reward of some kind or a big hug or a clap.

In order to ensure that feedback is effective we have to abide by these rules:

1. The medium you use must be meaningful

This will depend upon the individual child. A pre-verbal child may fail to appreciate a verbal message, especially when it is given in a monotonous voice. He may respond to the tone of voice. If tangible feedback is used it must be something which the child really enjoys. This is true of any kind of feedback. Some children enjoy a big hug and others respond better to a smile.

2. The contrast must be clear

We have to make a clear distinction between our actions when a child is doing what we want, and those when he is not.

For instance, if we frequently use 'good boy' as general encouragement and also use 'good boy' as feedback, the child will not get the message. Similarly, when we give him a sweet for getting something right, but also pop a sweet in his mouth at other times, this too is not clear feedback.

When carrying out a teaching task we must exaggerate the contrast between what happens when he gets something RIGHT and what happens when it is WRONG.

For instance, a child might be learning to feed. When he gets the food on his spoon and gets it to his mouth, we turn to him and smile and say 'good'. When he starts to mess about with the food, we turn away, ignore him and say nothing. The difference between the two actions is obvious and this will help the child to understand what is wanted.

3. Immediacy

Feedback must always be given *immediately* the child performs the correct action. This is harder than it sounds and the teacher must be very alert.

Imagine you are helping a child with a formboard game. You have named an object and want the child to put it into the right place. He does this, but you are not watching, and by the time you turn round and reward him he has got bored and is throwing the piece away. You have then rewarded *bad* behaviour instead of good.

4. Consistency

We all know we should be consistent, but this is an almost impossible ideal. Luckily, children eventually learn to deal with inconsistency. However, at the outset, when we are introducing a teaching game, consistency is vitally important.

At the outset, it is important to indicate that the child is correct, every time, and in the same way; and to ignore the incorrect choices. Once the behaviour has been established, then consistent feedback is not so important.

5. Task-centred feedback

It is sometimes much easier to be consistent if the feedback is built into the task. For instance, a posting box with different shaped blocks to be posted into the holes has its own built-in feedback. Only when a child fits the block into the right hole does he have the satisfaction of hearing it fall into the box.

With task-centred feedback, the child can play and learn on his own without being dependent upon an adult.

6. More success than failure

When learning a new task, a child will obviously not get it right every time. However, unless he is more often right than wrong he will find it difficult to learn what is expected of him.

Initially, you may have to use prompts as well as feedback, i.e. help him do the task and then praise him immediately for getting it right. Once he has got the idea, the prompts can be faded out.

Summary

These are the points to remember when giving feedback:

(1) use a medium which is meaningful for THAT child;
(2) make a clear distinction between positive and negative feedback;
(3) give immediate feedback;
(4) aim at task-centred feedback whenever possible;
(5) be consistent;
(6) ensure success by linking your feedback to prompts.

Conclusions

In this chapter we have described specific skills a teacher can use to:

(a) get the child's attention and retain his interest;
(b) show the child what is expected of him;
(c) grade her demands on the child;
(d) give the child feedback.

But reading about them is not enough. The only way a teacher can acquire these skills is through trying them out with children.

7 : Learning through Spontaneous Play

In the introduction to this section, and also in our book, *Let Me Play*, we have referred to the amazing number of basic skills which children can normally develop in the first few years of life through play. This is particularly true of skills which are pre-requisites to further learning, i.e. eye-hand co-ordination, mobility, imitation, etc.

However, some handicapping conditions are characterised by the failure for such spontaneous play to develop. If their development is not to be stunted, these handicapped children have to be shown how to play in a structured situation. Our 'Let Me' books describe how this can be done.

However, this is not enough. We also need to encourage more independent and spontaneous play so that the children can not only consolidate the skills they have learnt in the structured situation, but also take them further by combining different skills. Further, if they are to learn independence, such play is essential.

This chapter suggests how such spontaneous play may be fostered.

FAVOURABLE CONDITIONS FOR SPONTANEOUS PLAY

1. Freedom from undue stress

A child is unlikely to play unless his basic bodily needs have been met. Undernourished children play very little. Cold, bodily discomfort or extreme frustration will reduce the incidence of play.

2. The presence of a tolerant adult

Although we are concentrating on spontaneous and child-initiated play, this does not mean that it is independent of adult encouragement. There are certain cultures where there is apparently very little spontaneous play in childhood, possibly because the children are expected very early in life to take part in the real work of the community.

A tolerant and sympathetic adult gives young children the courage to play. She provides a buffer and protects the child from the traumas and dangers inherent in exploration.

A young child will often play happily while his mother is in the room and 'freeze up' in the presence of strangers.

While not initiating the play, the adult should be willing to be drawn into the child's play. She will also provide an appreciative audience and a source of toys or materials.

Lack of tolerance on the part of the adult may blight a child's attempts—he will be made to feel 'inept' and be unwilling to have another go.

3. Opportunities to imitate adult activities

Observation of children will convince one that play is often modelled on adults at work.

Think of typical 'pretence' play. (The importance of this kind of play has been outlined in our 'Let Me' books.) Children play 'mothers and fathers'; 'schools' or 'doctors'.

As we have already outlined in our 'Let Me' books, a handicapped child has often less opportunity to watch parents and others at work than a normal child. It is important to provide these opportunities. Again the adult needs to be tolerant enough to allow the child to have 'a finger in the pie', however inconvenient this may be.

The presence of suitable toys (toy ironing boards, hoovers, etc.) may also stimulate a handicapped child to copy his elders in spontaneous play.

4. The right toys at the right time

Although we are concerned with self-initiated play, the adult who is tuned in to the child's wave-length can often help to trigger off, sustain or develop such playing if she uses her imagination by producing appropriate toys or materials at the crucial moment. A doll's teaset may trigger off social play, for instance.

5. A few toys at a time

Watching a young child at Christmas time will help one to appreciate the fact that he can be overwhelmed by having too many toys to play with. He is spoilt for choice. A limited but developmentally appropriate collection of toys is more likely to result in spontaneous play.

6. Freedom to experiment

Many educational toys do not lend themselves to creativity. There is a 'proper' way to put rings on a ring-stack or solve a jig-saw puzzle, for instance.

In a free-play situation, we should not be over-concerned when children do not use these toys in the 'proper' way. A child at a certain stage of development may indeed learn something by completing a ring-stack or a puzzle properly, but he may learn even more if he is sometimes allowed to experiment with the rings—i.e. try them on his fingers, feed them to his doll, or use them as hoops for instance.

Teachers need to be flexible in this respect. One sometimes hears adults who are trying to interest a child in a toy, saying, 'Stop playing about'. Yet surely this is just what toys are for!

7. Freedom to make your own rules

A handicapped child is often at a disadvantage in his attempt to adapt to his life situation. One reason is that the 'rules of the game' are nearly always made by someone else.

A child who constantly fails to appreciate these rules or come up to an adult standard can become most disheartened and opt out.

Play is a safety valve. A child, playing on his own, cannot fail because he makes his own rules to fit his capacities, and may be constantly changing the rules of the game! This does not, in practice, mean that he is always making his game too easy and not making an effort. Watch, for instance, a child teaching himself to skip. He will make immense efforts, but if real skipping is, at present beyond his capacity, he will make do with pseudo-skipping. That is, he will exercise some of the skills needed for real skipping—turning the rope perhaps, or jumping, but not over the rope.

When he is ready and has practiced them all separately, he will be ready for *real* skipping!

8. A responsive playmate

A child's first playmate is his mother. Mother and child will have established a playful, non-verbal dialogue long before language develops.

In this kind of play, the parent is always following the child's lead, although she may gradually introduce variations and add intentionality into the game. For instance, by a mother's responding to a child's random vocalisations, they become intentional and increasingly precise. The importance of such playful dialogue cannot be over-emphasised.

Later a child will initiate playful interaction with other responsive adults and children.

9. Responsive environment

A child with very limited physical or mental capacities will often become rather passive when he is left to his own devices. It is not always possible to provide a responsive person for him to play with. But with a little ingenuity one is often able to rig up a responsive environment. A very young baby will learn to amuse himself if, for instance, one end of a string is attached to his arm and the other end attached to a mobile.

10. Freedom from interference

It is important to resist the temptation to interfere every time a handicapped child begins to play on his own.

He will not develop spontaneous play unless he is **given**

breathing spaces in which he is free from such adult direction and can experiment on his own.

One of the characteristics of spontaneous play is that it is carried out for its own sake and not for any extrinsic reward.

Summary

In this book we hàve already stressed the importance of structured one-to-one learning situations for a handicapped child's development. This chapter underlines also the importance of providing the child with favourable conditions in which he can practice his new-found skills through independent play.

Optimal conditions for spontaneous play are characterised by:

(1) freedom from undue stress;
(2) the presence of a tolerant adult;
(3) opportunities to imitate adult activities;
(4) the right toys at the right time;
(5) a few toys at a time;
(6) freedom to experiment;
(7) freedom to make his own rules;
(8) a responsive environment;
(10) freedom from interference.

SECTION 3: ASSESSING PROGRESS

Introduction

Once you have decided upon your objective and teaching methods, and you have started to carry them out, then any further decisions you make will be based on one main consideration: an assessment of the child's progress.

If the child has progressed, i.e. your objective has been achieved

Seeing a child progress is probably the best reward for all your hard work. It is also a great confidence booster. It confirms that your choice of objective and teaching methods were appropriate and that the way you carried out the teaching really did help the child to learn.

Once you are satisfied that your objective has been achieved you can start thinking about the next objective. This will be chosen in the same way as we described earlier (see Section 1).

If the child is making little or no progress

It is vitally important that you recognise this. If you continue to think that the child is progressing when in fact he is not, you will make no attempt to give the child the help he really needs.

Often, though, we are well aware that the child is not progressing, yet we do nothing about it. Indeed, we may even give up trying to help the child. In one sense this is understandable. You may have put such effort into the teaching that when you see no progress your enthusiasm wanes and your interest is not maintained. But it will not help the child if you stop teaching. Indeed, you will then be denying him the opportunity to learn.

You must do something about a child's lack of progress. We find it useful to ask ourselves the following questions:

1. Have we given the child enough time?

One is often disappointed when there is no *immediate* sign of progress. Yet we have found with mentally handicapped children that it is quite common for there to be little progress over the first week or so of daily sessions. This may be because these children need more time to get used to the new demands you are making of them. The danger is that you may give up just when the child is ready to show some progress. So if he is co-operative and interested, and is trying, albeit without success, it could well be that all he needs is more time. However, we hasten to add that this is rarely the sole answer. There are other important questions to consider. But before you make any changes, you have to be confident that you have given the child enough time.

2. Are we hindering the child's learning?

In any teaching situation there are two people involved: a teacher and a learner. The behaviour of one almost invariably affects the behaviour of the other. Thus a child's lack of progress has to be evaluated against the teaching received. It could well be that the teacher has been unintentionally *hindering*, rather than helping, the child's learning. This is quite a common reason for a child's lack of progress, especially, but not exclusively, when the teacher is relatively inexperienced. We shall examine this in some detail in Chapter 9 (page 137).

3. Are we using the most suitable method?

The reason for the lack of progress may lie in the method you are using. The child may be uninterested in your 'game', or you may have chosen an inappropriate method of prompting or giving feedback. Indeed, you may be trying to teach two things at the same time, with the result that the child learns neither (see page 97).

Some signs which suggest an inappropriate method are:

(i) the child gets repeatedly stuck at the same point
or (ii) he continually makes the same error,
or (iii) the child loses interest in the task.

If you suspect that your method is at fault—try another. Often there are several ways of achieving the same end.

4. Is our objective too advanced?

If the child can still do only part of the task, even after you have tried various methods, then it could well be that your objective is too advanced. You then need to re-appraise your objective. By now you will have obtained a lot of information about the child and will be in a much better position than you were at the beginning to choose a more appropriate objective. For example, if you had presumed that the child had certain pre-requisite skills which in fact he lacks, then your objective may now be to help him develop these skills.

5. Could there be other reasons for the lack of progress?

With the vast majority of children, the first four questions should help you to pinpoint the reasons for lack of progress, so that you can take appropriate action. However, with some children there may be other reasons for their failure to progress:

(1) Profoundly handicapped children with *severe* physical as well as intellectual handicaps may show no progress even after hours spent teaching them. Or what progress there is may be very minimal. Even very small gains can be major achievements for these children.

(2) Some children may need to take drugs which can affect their ability to learn. There is a very useful booklet called *A Teacher's Guide to Drugs* which describes the effects on children's behaviour of the more common drugs. This is obtainable from the National Council for Special Education, 1 Wood Street, Stratford-upon-Avon, CV37 6JE.

(3) With other children, their handicap may be of a progressive nature, i.e. it gets worse with time. If this is the case, your efforts may need to be directed at stopping the child from regressing and losing the skills he already has, rather than at teaching new skills. In such situations, no change can be a real achievement.

Accurate and detailed assessment

However, if your assessment of the child's progress is to inform your teaching, it is vital that it is both accurate and detailed.

If you say the child is progressing, when in fact he is not (or vice versa), then your future decisions will very likely be wrong.

If you say, 'he's definitely improving', although this may be accurate, it will not guide you as to the action you should now take.

With handicapped children there are special problems because there is no readily available 'yardstick' to use. With normal children we usually take a child's age as a guide to progress: thus if a child learns to walk by eleven months, we rightly say that he is making good progress. But if a child is mentally or physically handicapped, then his age is no longer a reliable or appropriate yardstick. We have to create another.

In this section we shall examine some methods which teachers can use to make an accurate and detailed assessment of children's progress. We have divided the section into two chapters:

Chapter 8—Describes various methods for assessing a child's progress, based mainly on observations. The importance of record keeping is stressed, and various methods for doing this are examined.

Chapter 9—Outlines some of the common ways in which teachers (particularly inexperienced teachers) can unconsciously hinder a child's learning, and then describes how these can be identified and overcome.

In the two appendices linked with this chapter, we describe a detailed method for assessing teachers' behaviour (Appendix 1), and look particularly at language-learning situations, for here the adult's role is especially crucial to successful learning (Appendix 2).

8 : Assessing the Child's Progress

In this chapter we shall describe various methods you can use to assess a child's progress, both in the short-term and in the long-term. As we stressed in the Introduction, the aim of this assessment is to help you improve your teaching. We shall therefore concentrate on assessment methods which are:

(*a*) directly linked with the teaching situation;
(*b*) quick and easy to carry out;
(*c*) accurate and informative.

Finally, we shall examine ways of keeping records of the child's progress to which you and *others* can refer.

However, we must stress that we envisage these assessments as taking place primarily in the context of individual teaching schemes linked with specific objectives. We realise that there are many other aspects of teaching which are not so amenable to the methods of assessment we describe here. This is not to imply that we should make no attempt to assess progress in such areas, but that we need to explore other ways to enable us to do so.

Impressions can be misleading

Very often, teachers form their own impression as to whether a child is making progress or not. Such impressions may derive from their observations of the child and may well be accurate. However, we suspect that working solely on the basis of impressions is unwise, for some or all of the following reasons:

(*a*) Impressions rely heavily on memory. You have to recall what the child was doing two weeks or even three months ago. Of course the longer the time span, the more difficult it is to recall accurately. Hence impressions can be distorted by memory.

(b) Although impressions may be accurate when striking changes have occurred in the child's behaviour (e.g. he can walk alone, where before he only crawled), it is much harder to form accurate impressions of small changes in the child's behaviour. The danger is that these are overlooked and we form the impression that no progress has been made.

(c) Or conversely, we expect changes to occur and therefore we form the impression that they have occurred, and thus that there has been progress, when in fact there has been none.

Therefore we have to conclude that impressions are rarely *sufficiently* detailed and accurate to be really informative. We need to back up our impressions by pinpointing more precisely the change or changes in the child.

METHODS OF ASSESSING PROGRESS

We want to make a distinction between two approaches to assessing progress, although in practice the distinction can become rather blurred.

1. Before/After

Here you compare the child's behaviour before you embark upon teaching activities, with his behaviour after the activities have been in use for a period of time. Periodic assessments of the child (e.g. six-monthly or yearly) also fall into this category.

2. On-going

As the name implies, progress is here assessed while the teaching activities are being carried out. Thus the person doing the teaching is invariably the assessor of progress. This need not be the case with the Before/After method, in which case an 'outsider' can assess progress.

We shall consider each approach in turn.

Before/After assessments

In education, but particularly in educational research, before/after assessments are frequently carried out using standardised tests, such as the Griffith Test of Mental Development or the Reynell Language Development Scales. Such tests are rarely useful to the teacher interested in assessing progress, however, for they do not relate directly to her teaching situation. So she will often have to devise her own methods of assessment. Now this sounds more difficult than it actually is, and in this part of the chapter we shall illustrate just how easy it can be to devise your own methods.

Your methods, if they are to be useful, should embody two of the characteristics of tests:

(*a*) The assessment should yield systematic and precise measures. This means that:

   (i) you can detect quite small improvements;

  (ii) different children's progress can be compared;

 (iii) the same assessments can be carried out by different people;

 (iv) you have a common 'language' for talking about the child with other professionals.

(*b*) The emphasis should be on observing, not on teaching.

Measures of progress. In order to assess progress objectively you will need to have a precise measure. A test, after all, is only a sophisticated measure. The problem is that there is no one measure that you can always use to assess progress. The measure has to vary according to the progress you want to assess. This means that the most appropriate measure often derives directly from your teaching objective, for this sets out the change you expect to see in the child (see Chapter 3).

Your objective provides your measure. For example, with one of the children, Tommy, our objective was to encourage him to use the verbs 'eat', 'sit' and 'kick' appropriately in expressive language. This objective was chosen after we had analysed

Tommy's expressive language over a number of sessions and found that his expressive language consisted mainly of nouns and very few verbs. These are the *before* sessions (see Chapter 2 for further details as to how this is done).

We then embarked upon some specific teaching games with Tommy (see *Let Me Speak*, page 90, for details), and after four weeks we reviewed his progress. The measure we used was the number of times Tommy used the verbs 'eat', 'sit' and 'kick'. Figure 8 shows the big improvement that had occurred. Conversely, with another child, Claire, exactly the same games over the same period did not result in any improvement. With her it was another four weeks before we saw any improvement.

NAME: *Tommy and Claire*
OBJECTIVE: *Appropriate use of verbs; eat, sit and kick in expressive language*
SITUATION: *Doll play*   LENGTH OF SESSIONS: *6 minutes*

	Before	*After (4 weeks)*	*After (a further 4 weeks)*
Tommy	11	1111 1111 1111 1111 1111 11	1111 1111 1111 1111 1111 1111 1111 1111
Total	2	27	39
Claire	1111	1111 1111	1111 1111 1111 1111 1111 1111 11
Total	4	9	32

Figure 8. Frequency Checklist used with Tommy and Claire

Thus the measures of frequency, duration, etc. which we described in Chapter 2 (see page 35) can also be used to assess progress. The important point to remember is:

Choose the measure which most closely reflects your objective. For example, with another child, Jane, our objective was to get her to place rings on a ring-stack. Thus our measure could have been the number of times she successfully placed a ring on the stack. However, in itself, that could have been misleading.

During the *before* session she had six successes and *after* the teaching this had increased only to eight. Seemingly little improvement, until you take into account that the six successes in the *before* session were out of 18 attempts—a 33% success rate, whereas *after*, the eight successes were out of ten attempts —80% success rate. 'Percentage success' was a more appropriate measure of our objective.

Equally, you may over-estimate progress if you choose the wrong measure. In our earlier example with Claire, we could have counted all the times she said the three verbs, whether appropriately or inappropriately. Since the count itself had clearly increased, we might have concluded that she had progressed. But in our objective, we had specified that the verbs would be used *appropriately* (see page 121). Therefore our measure had to reflect this.

Advantages of precise measures. With every specific teaching objective specific measures can be devised to assess progress. You have only to decide which particular measure, e.g. frequency, duration, variety, etc., is best suited to your objective. You use this measure to record the child's behaviour before you embark on the teaching (we described how you could do this in Chapter 2), and then you repeat the whole exercise after a certain number of teaching sessions. This will help to confirm and elaborate your impressions of the child's progress.

The main advantages of using a precise measure are:

(i) *You can detect quite small improvements.* At times, the amount of progress may be small and could go undetected (cf. Claire). But seeing some progress will encourage you to continue the teaching for a bit longer, rather than change it, or give up.

(ii) *You can compare different children's progress.* The measure gives you a precise way of describing differences between children (cf. Tommy and Claire).

(iii) *The same assessment can be carried out by different people.* It is a great morale booster for a teacher to have the success of her teaching confirmed by an 'outsider'. This is especially so with parents who are working in partnership with professionals (see Chapter 10). Here the professional may see the parents and the child only on a monthly basis (e.g. pre-school child, page 19). In such cases, it is very important for the parent and professional to have a common measure of progress.

(iv) *It provides a common language for talking about the child with other professionals.* You can convey more precise information about the child, your teaching and the resultant progress with the help of such measures (see Chapter 11).

Observe, don't teach. However, there is another characteristic of the 'testing' approach which we should also try to embody in our before/after methods, and that is summed up in the maxim: 'observe, don't teach'. We stressed the importance of this in making an accurate appraisal of the child's abilities (see Chapter 2). It is equally important that you carry this over into the assessment session *after* the teaching. Here there is a great temptation for a teacher to continue to give the child help, by modelling, with prompts or even just by eye-gaze! If you do this, you will not get a true indication of the child's learning.

So just as when giving a preliminary test, the teacher's role should be that of an observer; merely noting what the child does and neither helping nor responding to the child, except to give general encouragement.

We realise that this is much easier said than done. One way to try to achieve these conditions is by observing the child attempting the task without adult supervision (one-way screens are very useful for this). Sometimes we pretend to be busy with something else and leave the child to get on with it. You may be able to devise your own ways. However, the important point to remember is that there are times when you need to stop teaching so that you can take stock of what you have achieved, and plan what to do next.

Summary. A before/after assessment based on precise measures, is an easy yet informative method of assessing a child's progress. It is economical in terms of time, but can also provide quite a stringent test of the child's learning.

On-going assessment

Assessment of progress is not only carried out on a before/after basis. It can, and indeed should, be on-going throughout all the teaching sessions. The ability to make an accurate, on-going assessment of the child's progress is the hallmark of the experienced teacher. It requires a great deal of skill to assess the child's behaviour and adjust your demands in the light of your assessment. You have to make instant decisions; you have to be able to anticipate; you have to be flexible so that you can switch to other alternatives.

It is rather like driving a car (except that teaching can be far more unpredictable!). In order to keep the car safely on the road the driver has constantly to assess progress, anticipate dangers etc. It is no good assessing after the crash!

Yet, like driving, making an accurate on-going assessment while teaching is a skill that comes only with experience: that is, experience of the child's abilities and interests; experience in using teaching techniques; and experience in assessing yourself as a teacher (a topic we shall discuss in the next chapter).

Most of all, this ability develops through the experience of critically assessing your own teaching sessions. And it is this aspect which we will concentrate on here.

Making a record. It is very hard to remember accurately all that went on during a teaching session. A recording of the session is very useful, especially if you want to make a detailed examination of it.

A video-tape recording is the ideal, of course, although in many cases an audio-recording will do nearly as well. Indeed, cassette recorders have some advantages in that they are more compact and less likely to distract the child.

Here are two tips gained from our experience. First, try not to let the child see you working with the recorder. Have it set up and running before you start the teaching with the child, and wait until he is away from the teaching area before switching it off.

Second, identify each session by saying at the beginning the name of the child, the date and teaching objective. With audio-tape it is also useful to note the equipment which was available.

Analysing the record. The first priority is to make an analysis of the child's behaviour. (You can also use the recording to analyse yourself, as we will discuss in Chapter 9.) There are two main aspects to this: (*a*) analysis of 'errors', and (*b*) target behaviour, i.e. the child does what we want him to do, as summarised in our objective.

(*a*) *Analysis of 'errors'.* The purpose of this analysis is to pinpoint those aspects of the task on which the child is 'failing', so that you can adjust your teaching accordingly. However, as the following examples will show, words such as 'errors' or 'failing' are being used in a very wide sense. It would perhaps be more appropriate to think not in terms of errors, but of stages of learning. An example will make this clearer.

With Mark, our objective was to have him place rings on a simple ring-stack. Our main teaching 'method' was the use of a light and buzzer, which came on whenever he placed a ring on the stack (see *Let Me Play*, page 120). However, we did use modelling as well.

In order to summarise Mark's actions during the teaching session, we prepared a checklist (see Figure 9) of the different stages in the ring-stacking task. This was divided into columns. A new column was used each time he lifted a ring. On playing back the recording we were then able to note the stages he could do and those which he failed to do, plus any other 'unrelated' actions, such as throwing a ring, or knocking over the stack. From this analysis, we noted that Mark could search, grasp and position the ring, but had difficulty aligning it correctly to the top of the stack. When he could not get a ring on, he resorted to throwing it.

NAME: *Mark*   DATE: *31st May*   LENGTH OF SESSION: *10 minutes*
Place a tick against the item if the child successfully does it
Place a cross against the item if the child fails to do it

	1	2	3	4	5	6	7	8	9	10
Searches for ring	√	√	√	√	√			√	√	√
Grasps ring with finger and thumb	√	√	√	√				√	√	√
Positions ring at top of stack	√	×	√	√				√	√	√
Aligns ring to stack	×		√	×				×	×	×
Releases ring on stack	×		√	×						
Other items:										
Throwing rings	×	×		×	×	×	×	×	×	×
Knocks stack over				×			×			

Figure 9. Checklist for Ring-stacking Task

We then decided to use physical prompts as an additional technique to help him align the ring correctly. However, these were used only at that point. He could carry out all the other stages by himself, so there was no need to use physical prompts for these.

With time, these prompts were gradually removed and Mark learnt to do the ring-stacking task.

But not all tasks lend themselves to such a 'stage' analysis. For instance, in teaching expressive language you need to use a rather different type of checklist, although the rationale is still the same, that is, it pinpoints aspects of the task on which the child might need specific help.

For example, Figure 10 shows the checklist we used with Tommy and Claire (see earlier). Our objective, you recall, was

E

NAME: *Tommy*

OBJECTIVE: *Appropriate use of verbs, eat (E), sit (S) and kick (K)* in *expressive language*

Words used		Totals
	E E E E	Eat – 4
Spontaneous		Sit – 0
and		Kick – 0
appropriate		
	S S S K S S S E K K S K	
Spontaneous		Eat – 1
but		Sit – 7
Inappropriate		Kick – 4
	K K E E S S K E S K K K S S S	
Direct	K E E	Eat – 5
imitation		Sit – 6
		Kick – 7
Unclear	1111 1111 1	11

Figure 10. Checklist for Expressive Language

to encourage appropriate use of the verbs, 'eat', 'sit' and 'kick'. In the session analysed, Tommy imitated all the verbs, but he was using only 'eat' spontaneously and appropriately. Therefore in subsequent teaching sessions we no longer concentrated on imitations, but tried to encourage him to say the words by himself, e.g. by using prompts, such as 'Tommy ....' (leaving him to add the verb). A subsequent teaching session can likewise be analysed to see if this new technique is proving effective. If it is not, then other methods will have to be tried (see *Let Me Speak* for further examples).

(*b*) *Target behaviour.* This analysis is very similar to the before/after method, for here too you note the number of times, or length of time, the child shows the behaviour which you are aiming for, except that you now do this analysis for each teaching session. This analysis can serve a number of purposes:

(i) *You will be able to detect learning trends.* Sometimes, when progress is slow, one session may not appear very different from the next. Yet over a period of, say, ten sessions, a gradual change may have taken place which you were not really aware of: that is, there is a 'learning' trend.

Conversely, the child's behaviour may fluctuate from session to session, giving the impression that he is learning when really there is no definite trend (see Figure 11).

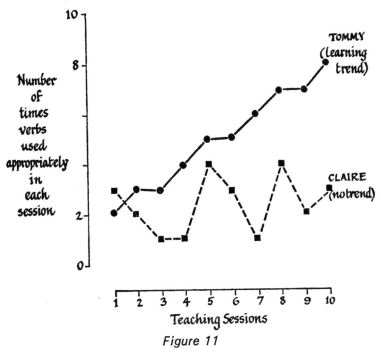

Figure 11

(ii) *It will give you encouragement.* You as a teacher need encouragement, just as much as the child. We get ours from seeing a child progress. One good way of highlighting the child's progress is by drawing a *cumulative* graph. This graph is unusual in that it is in fact a running total of the number of times the child shows the target behaviour. For example, with Tommy, the number of times he used three new verbs appropriately over the first six teaching sessions was as follows:

Teaching session	Number of verbs	Cumulative count
1	2	2
2	2	4
3	1	5
4	4	9
5	6	15
6	10	25

When drawn as a graph (Figure 12), with the sessions on the horizontal axis and the cumulative count on the

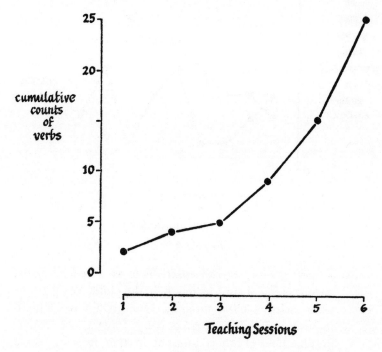

Figure 12

vertical axis, there is a clear visual record of Tommy's progress; the graph rising gently at first then steeply. If there is no progress at all, the graph remains flat.

(iii) *It gives you a permanent record of your teaching.* An on-going analysis, especially in the form of a graph, is an excellent record of the child's progress which can easily be understood by others. It is easy and quick to prepare and saves a great number of words!

Recording during the teaching session. Thus far we have suggested that the analysis of the child's behaviour is done from a recording of the teaching session. However, it is of course possible to make an analysis *during* the session, as long as you know in advance what you are looking for. And here the checklists can be particularly useful, because the teacher can use them during the teaching session. This, however, can be rather distracting to the child, and it means that the teacher cannot concentrate solely on the child. Ideally, another person should act as 'observer' and fill in the checklist.

Doing it 'in your head'. Finally, we must stress that we are *not* suggesting that you analyse every teaching session in this way. That would be an impossibility. But it is possible to carry out an on-going assessment 'in your head'. As we said earlier, that is what the good teacher is constantly doing. To do this effectively, however, you have to have an idea of the main things to look out for. Here too, the checklists can be useful, for if you keep them in mind, you can mentally tick off those aspects in which the child needs help.

Summary. An on-going assessment should be an integral part of all our teaching. But it requires a great deal of skill on the part of the teacher. In order to develop that skill, we have suggested that teachers should first work from a recording of their teaching sessions, analysing the child's progress and pinpointing those aspects on which he requires particular help. Although rather time-consuming, it is an invaluable training exercise for the inexperienced teacher and can even prove to be an enlightening refresher course for the experienced teacher!

Long-term progress
Thus far we have concentrated on assessing the child's progress in the context of specific teaching objectives, and that means over a relatively short period of time. In the final part of this chapter, we will examine some ways teachers can use to record a child's long-term progress over his school career.

Record keeping. But before examining how you can keep records, it is worth asking *why*? Is it important? We think it is, and can give three good reasons.

Encouragement. With handicapped children progress is sometimes so slow, and our memories are so poor, that we can easily overlook or forget about the changes which have occurred. Reading back over your records can be a real source of encouragement.

Passing on information to others. Often many different people can be involved with a handicapped child. A written record is a very concise way of passing on information, either between professionals or from parents to professionals.

Records help you to plan ahead. Your short-term objectives are often only a means to an end, not an end in themselves. However, you can sometimes lose sight of this in the day-to-day teaching of the child. Your records should help to place your objectives in an overall context, so that you can continue to build upon past learning.

Methods of keeping records. We shall describe briefly three different methods for keeping records. These are not intended to be alternatives, since they complement each other, and where possible all three should be used.

Developmental Charts. These are a very concise and useful way of keeping an on-going record of the child's progress (see page 23). To do this, the teacher 'dates' the boxes when the child first shows the skill. The teacher would go through the charts every three months or so, to bring them up to date. This gives both a record of the child's present abilities, and a record of the child's progress: for example, it shows when he first started to use two words in expressive language, and the time which elapsed between this and when he was credited with four or five clear words.

Thus the Developmental Charts are a very useful way of recording the child's progress over a long period of time. They also provide a concise way of conveying information to others (see page 27).

Record Cards. One disadvantage of the Developmental Charts is that they are often not sufficiently detailed, which means that quite significant changes in the child's behaviour can be overlooked. In such instances, the charts need to be supplemented with more detailed records.

Figure 13 gives an example of how this can be done. There is a separate card for each 'area of development' in the Charts (see page 24). The main advantage of the cards is that you can see very easily how each objective links with the previous ones. You can even plan out in advance a series of objectives for the child. However, be prepared to make changes in the light of experience: you may need to add extra steps, while you may be able to delete others.

There is one danger of which we need to beware. That is, since your teaching is confined to specific areas of development, you must remember that this division into areas is only a useful way of structuring your observations and recording, not a general reflection of how the child is developing. Your objectives and/or teaching methods may involve a number of areas of development, not all of which are reflected in the cards. (See *Let Me Play* for a further discussion of this.)

Record cards, especially if linked with graphs or charts

RECORD CARD FOR LANGUAGE DEVELOPMENT
NAME: *Michael*   DATE OF BIRTH: *19.6.1970*

Objectives	Date		Comments
	Started	Ended	
To pick out correctly from an array of four objects: a ball, cup, car, teddy	25 March	19 April	Used 'Give Me game' (Let Me Speak, p. 106) with chocolate drops
As before, but with four new objects; spoon, bus, comb, dolly, making eight in all	20 April	30 April	Chocolate drops no longer needed
To use the words; ball, car, and teddy appropriately in posting games	20 April	26 May	Used both small objects and pictures. He will imitate but not use the words appropriately by himself
As before	27 May	13 June	Used picture form-board—Success!
To use words; spoon, bus, comb, as well as the previous three	17 June	20 June	Used form-boards and posting games. Still confuses car and bus occasionally

Figure 13. Record Card for Language Development

obtained from your assessment of the child's progress with each teaching objective, are the most detailed form of record-keeping, and therefore quite time-consuming. However, it will be time well spent as you will find it a real aid to further planning.

Diary. This could be done daily, although weekly may suffice. The main purpose of the diary format is to record significant events which occur rather unexpectedly or only occasionally. Figure 14 is an extract from one teacher's diary (a parent). The diary gives an intimate and personal account of the child's progress which is lacking in the previous two methods. It is a very useful complement to them.

Week beginning	
6th August	Angela can now pedal her tricycle uphill. For the past week she has stayed dry all night and last Wednesday even went to the bathroom by herself when she woke up.
13th August	Asked 'Who's that?' when we were talking about a friend. We thought she wasn't listening. That is the first time she has ever used that sort of question.
20th August	Angela is now using a knife and fork with most meals. Sometimes she tends to scoop her food on to her knife and eat off this, but generally she is improving. Continues to keep dry at night. Also started to use a new phrase quite a lot recently— 'Oh dearie me!' Uses it when there has been an accident or mishap.

Figure 14. An Example of a Parent's Diary

Finally, we may have given the impression that all these records should be neatly filed away in a folder kept in the teacher's desk. This may well be the best way to keep them, but equally, there is no reason why you should not keep some of your records in the form of large sheets placed up on the wall. For example, you may want to record all the words which a child uses in expressive language. You could pin up a sheet of paper in the classroom, so that you can immediately jot down any new word which you hear. The great advantage of this method is that others can be involved in the record-keeping too, e.g. assistants, volunteer helpers etc.

E*

Thus, for both convenience *and* involvement of others, don't keep all the records in your desk!

Concluding comment. Keeping detailed records does entail extra work for the teacher, and it requires a good deal of self-discipline to keep them up to date. But unless you have a systematic way of keeping records you will not do justice to all the hard work you have put into the teaching. Indeed, your efforts may well be forgotten, even by yourself.

9 : Assessing the Teacher

When a child learns a new skill, the teacher quite rightly takes a great deal of pride in the achievement: 'I taught him that', we say. However, we are less inclined to take the blame for the child's failure to learn. Instead, we tend to place the blame elsewhere, and usually it's on the child! When you think of it, this is rather a strange attitude to take. After all, the child did not ask to be taught. It was the teacher who decided on the objective and the methods. Yet when the child fails to learn, it's he who gets the blame!

Of course, it is easy to put the blame on to a child's handicap. We can say that the child did not learn because of his handicaps, conveniently forgetting that his handicap may, at least in part, be the result of our failure to help his learning.

Therefore when a child appears to be making little or no progress, we need first of all to examine ourselves as teachers. And often we find that unintentionally we have been hindering rather than helping the child's learning. But before we go on to describe *how* we may be hindering a child's learning, it is worth examining *why* we may be doing so. As we have been just as guilty as any other teachers of hindering, we would like to make a few points in our defence: a plea of mitigation you might say!

It is hard to observe yourself. At the best of times, it is difficult for us to stand back and see ourselves. How much more difficult, then, when you are with a child, organising materials, thinking about what to do next and maybe keeping an eye on other children at the same time.

We make wrong assumptions. There are no absolute rules when it comes to teaching a child. Therefore we have to work on the basis of assumptions, e.g. we assume a particular method works. In itself, this is not bad, but the danger is that we stick to our assumptions when they are proved wrong, and some of them are bound to be!

Perhaps this is best illustrated by an example. A father once told us that he believed the best way to stop his daughter from swearing was to smack her. He said he did this every time she swore, which was nearly every day. He then went on to say he had done this ever since she first swore two years ago! But if smacking worked, why was his daughter still swearing two years later? That father had made a wrong assumption, and he had stuck to it, ignoring all the evidence against its effectiveness.

We forget that only the child can do the learning. We are so eager to have the child learn that we tend to do all the work while the child watches! Yet you cannot make a child learn. All you can do is to help him. It is rather like taking the proverbial horse to water: you cannot do the drinking for it.

Thus our unintentional hindering often arises out of the best of intentions. But unless we identify and correct these mistakes we will not be effective teachers. So just as we need to examine the child, so too, we must learn to examine ourselves. The purpose of this examination is not just to find mistakes. You can also use it to check that your assumptions were right, and indeed you may even find instances where you have helped the child without realising it at the time.

First, though, we want to examine some of the main ways in which teachers can hinder a child's learning. Then we shall go on to describe how these can be spotted and changed.

TEACHER'S MISTAKES

In this section, we shall describe some of the common mistakes which we have come across, and outline briefly how they can be avoided. In fact all that we shall be doing is re-emphasising many of the points made in our earlier section on teaching methods (see page 85). This chapter is intended to complement that section, in that here we concentrate on *un*favourable learning conditions.

We shall focus on three mistakes, and illustrate them with tales of three teachers: the obedient teacher; the demanding teacher; and the confusing teacher. In case you think these are fairy tales, let us hasten to add that any resemblance to teachers living or dead is entirely deliberate!

Mistake 1: We do not have the child's attention

The child learns from you only when he is attending to you. Or to put it another way, you have to be in control. Yet too often we relinquish control to the child, with the result that instead of the child attending to us, we attend to the child. He decides what he is going to do and we obey!

The tale of the obedient teacher. This teacher wants Joe to thread beads on to a lace. Now Joe is a very active little boy, so while the teacher sits in the middle of the room, Joe is running around. As he does so, the teacher calls him, 'Joe, look what I've got; come and play with these'. This coaxing goes on for two or three minutes, but to no avail. By now Joe is rather tired of running, so instead he starts to climb up on a cupboard to reach some toys which are up on a shelf. The teacher, aware that he could fall and hurt himself, comes and lifts him down, carries him over to the beads and makes him sit on her knee. He struggles to get away, and though the teacher tries to restrain him, he manages to wriggle free. He heads straight for the cupboard and starts to climb it. The teacher tells him he must not do that and lifts him down again. Joe then makes for the beads and scatters them all over the floor. She tells him to pick them up again, but all he does is throw them.

She finally manages to collect the beads, by which time Joe is now trying to skip with the lace. Thankful that he's staying in one place, the teacher encourages him by saying, 'Oh that's good, you're skipping'. After a few minutes the teacher asks for the lace. Joe refuses and when she takes it, he throws such a temper tantrum that she has to give it back to shut him up.

We can safely say that this was not a very successful teaching session. The amount of time Joe spent on the required task was nil. In a successful session the child, ideally, should spend 100% of the time 'on the task', although a small percentage of 'off task' time is acceptable.

So where did our obedient teacher go wrong, and what could she have done instead?

Attended to undesirable behaviour. When Joe ran around, she talked to him, trying to coax him to play with the beads. When he climbed up on to the cupboard, she went and lifted him down. When he threw the beads, she picked them up, and when he skipped with the lace, she encouraged him. Joe was in control all the time and she acknowledged this, for he had her undivided attention even when he was ignoring her!

The solution? Do what Joe was doing—*ignore him when he is not doing the required task, but attend to him when he does.*

But you might then say that you cannot always ignore a child, especially when he could hurt himself, for example climbing. If that is the case, then lift him down but say nothing, act coldly to him, and be as impassive as possible.

Beware, too, of the very subtle ways children have of distracting you, like using the material in another way to the one you intended, e.g. the skipping with the lace. (Incidentally, the teacher had been trying to teach Joe to skip the day before.) But this was not the time for skipping practice and Joe needs to learn that. Skipping too should be ignored (see page 93).

What a boring game! The teacher made no attempt to make the threading appear interesting or enjoyable. Joe had to do it simply because the teacher said so! In fact, she did not even show him how to thread the beads on to the lace. It's not surprising that he threw the beads and skipped with the lace. He had been shown nothing else.

Rather the teacher should have modelled the threading and made it appear an exciting new game (see page 94).

Too many distractions. As the beads appeared so uninteresting, lots of other things caught Joe's attention. Things like— plenty of space to run around in, furniture to climb on, other toys to play with.

If the child is easily distracted, put away other toys and play in a more confined area. In short, remove distractions (see page 77).

They came into conflict. On two occasions the teacher and Joe came into direct conflict, making him sit on her knee and the taking of the lace.

The outcome of these situations is rarely satisfactory and usually the child wins in the end, in this case with the temper tantrum. The answer is to avoid confrontation. If you cannot get control, then pack up. That is the ultimate in ignoring (see page 93).

Mistake 2: We make too many demands
When we have got the child's attention we sometimes let the power go to our heads and we make one demand after another. This is certainly a mistake when the child is not capable of fulfilling them, either because there are so many different demands, or because they are at too high a level.

The tale of the demanding teacher. This teacher's objective was to have Paul learn to put three different shapes into the appropriate holes of a posting-box. Unlike Joe, Paul is a very passive child and is only too eager to please the teacher. This is what happened.

Teacher says	*Paul's actions*
Put the square one in	Paul puts the square in the box, then lifts a triangle
Now put the ball in	Tries to put the triangle in the box
No, a ball, I said. Put that one down	Drops the triangle on the floor
Go and pick it up	Paul lifts a ball and goes to post it
No, first pick that piece off the floor	Gets down from chair and fetches piece
Now sit up, sit up properly	Holds the triangle
Now show me a ball	Lifts a ball
Bring your chair nearer the table	Paul obeys
Now show me a triangle	Tries to post the ball
Put the ball down	Paul obeys
Now give me a square	Lifts the ball again.

As you can see, not much progress was made and here are some reasons why.

Changing demands. The teacher was not making clear to the child what she wanted him to do with the posting-box.

When the child made a mistake, the teacher started to make new demands and many different ones at that. These were (in order) not to hold the piece; to fetch them off the floor; to show her a certain piece; to give her a certain piece. In all, the child was asked to do five different things with the pieces and only one of these was directly related to the objective ('put the ball in the box'). The odds were five to one against the child guessing what he was expected to do with the material.

The teacher should have made only the posting demand, and no others (see page 96).

Irrelevant demands. Not only did she make different demands based around the pieces and the posting-box, but she also made three other demands which were irrelevant and would only distract the child from the task. These were:

> To get down from the table and fetch a fallen piece (as there were plenty of other pieces on the table, this could have been ignored).
> To sit up properly (the objective was not to improve the child's posture!).
> To bring the chair nearer (let the child decide for himself whether he needs to be nearer the table).

Fortunately, the remedy is simple—*cut out irrelevant demands.*

Failure to follow the child's lead. This is perhaps the most serious of all. The teacher was so demanding that she ignored what the child was doing.

> For example, on three occasions Paul tried to post an object, yet the teacher stopped him. First when he tried to post the triangle and she had said, 'ball'. This seems reasonable until you realise that he had lifted the triangle *before* she made the demand. So instead of encouraging him by saying, 'Yes, put the triangle in', she expected him to put the triangle down, find a ball and then post that. Three extra demands, all because she ignored what Paul had already done.
>
> On the next two occasions he was not allowed to post the pieces because the teacher had made new demands of fetching and showing her a piece. Thus the teacher made it doubly difficult for the child by changing her demands and ignoring his efforts at posting.

Therefore you need to *watch the child and take your lead from what he does, tailor your demands to his actions* (see page 111).

> You may wonder then why we thought the obedient teacher should have ignored Joe's skipping (see page 140). The reason is simply that the skipping was not related, nor

could it be easily related to the desired task. But that was not the case with Paul.

Mistake 3: We confuse right and wrong

If we want the child to do a particular thing, then we have to make very clear to him the difference between what it is we want him to do, and what we do not want him to do. If we fail to make the difference clear, then we will only confuse the child.

The tale of the confusing teacher. Kevin is a severely retarded child with no physical handicaps. His play is very immature and his teacher has been trying to encourage him to play properly with three objects, doll, cup and comb, instead of destroying them, which is what he often does with objects.

Teacher says	*Kevin's actions*
	Hitting doll against chair
Don't hit dolly against the chair, that's a good boy	
Give dolly a drink	Kevin puts the cup over the doll's mouth
No, do it properly, hold the cup by the handle	Kevin throws the cup and by chance it falls into the toy-box
Gosh you are clever, but you must not throw things	
Look, here's a comb	Kevin takes comb and briefly combs doll, then puts the comb in his mouth
A comb is not for eating	Kevin continues to chew the comb

Again, not a successful teaching session; probably because of the following reasons:

Appropriate behaviour ignored. On the two occasions Kevin played appropriately with the toys, the teacher either ignored it (the combing) or told him, 'No, that's not right' (doll and cup). It should have been 'Yes, well done' on both occasions.

You have to reinforce appropriate behaviour immediately, taking notice of it as soon as it occurs (it may not last for long) (see page 106).

Inappropriate behaviour is reinforced. Instead, the teacher comments on Kevin's inappropriate actions and even says, 'That's a good boy' and 'You are clever'! *These actions should be ignored.*

The child is told not to do things. With an immature child who may not understand language very well, the difference between 'A comb's not for eating' and 'A comb's for eating' is not very obvious. Yet the intended meaning is very different. Thus if Kevin does not understand the meaning of 'not', he will hear the teacher say 'Hit the dolly against the chair' and 'A comb's for eating'. When he does these actions, he is not being a naughty boy, in fact, just the opposite—he's doing what he thought the teacher told him to do!

Thus, avoid telling the child not to do something. It is much better simply to say 'No' or 'Stop it'.

However, there is another good reason for avoiding the word 'not', and that is because immature children find it very difficult to stop or inhibit their actions. They are very much more inclined towards actions, and when they hear you say something which sounds like a command, they will then tend to act.

In part this may be due to habit: for example, if you look at an open door and say to the child 'Don't close the door' it's likely that he will go and close it, because the context of the utterance is the same as when you do want him to close the door.

The moral of all this is best summed up by the old song— 'you've got to accentuate the positive, eliminate the negative'.

Concluding comment

Although we have used three separate examples to illustrate some common mistakes, we want to stress they can all occur in any teaching situation, with any child and with any teacher. We therefore need to examine ourselves so that we can identify our weaknesses, but at the same time also note our strengths.

EXAMINING THE TEACHER

There are two ways in which this can be done: (1) self-examination or (2) guided examination.

At the beginning of this chapter we pointed out that one of the main reasons why teachers unintentionally hinder the children's learning is the difficulty of observing oneself when teaching.

If we could see ourselves, we would spot our mistakes. Now, with the help of a recording (either audio-tape or video-tape), you can do just that. For this 'permanent' record lets you analyse yourself and the child's reactions in detail. We shall refer to this as *self-examination*.

However, with inexperienced teachers, a self-examination may not be very helpful; largely because they may not know what to look for. They would benefit more if they could examine themselves under the guidance of a more experienced teacher. We shall refer to this as a *guided examination*.

We shall now outline how these 'examinations' can be carried out.

Self-examination
So much happens in even the shortest teaching session that you need to have a recording if you are to carry out a self-examination. Video-tape is the ideal, for this gives you both sound and picture. In many cases, however, an audio-recording will do nearly as well (see earlier comments in Chapter 2, page 44). Indeed, with an audio-tape recorder you do not feel that you are being watched to the same extent as with video-tape.

This is how we carry out a self-examination from a recording:

1. Play back the recording immediately after the teaching session
Try to play back the recording as soon as possible after the

teaching session. This is especially important with audio-tape recordings, for here you have to remember what happened. Therefore the sooner you play the recording, the more chance you have of remembering correctly.

2. Know what you are looking for

This is one of the cardinal rules of any observation activity. Earlier we pinpointed many of the common mistakes which teachers can make. These, along with examples of desirable behaviour derived from Section 3, can be made into a simple checklist which will help you to guide your observations.

For example, you may be interested to look at the number of demands you made on the child. Prepare a simple checklist such as in Figure 15a, and every time you make a demand of the child, place a tick. Even just a count of the total number of demands can be an enlightening experience.

(a) COUNT OF DEMANDS

Demands   1111   1111   1111   1111

LENGTH OF SESSION: *2 minutes*

(b) TASK RELATED DEMANDS

Task related demands		1111	1111	11		32%
Task unrelated demands	1111	1111	1111	1111	111	68%

LENGTH OF SESSION: *8 minutes*

(c) TYPE OF DEMAND

(N.B. The checklist could be used by the 'demanding teacher' described earlier, see page 141)

OBJECTIVE: *To have child post piece in appropriate hole of posting-box.*

Put piece in posting-box	1111				10%
Give teacher a particular piece	1111	1			12%
Show teacher a particular piece	1111	1111			20%
Say the name of a particular piece	1111	1111	1111	11	34%
Other demands	1111	1111	11		24%

Note: This teacher's demands did not match her objective

Figure 15. Checklists for Self-Examination

However, you can make it more detailed by noting whether the demands were task-related or task-unrelated (see Figure 15b). Now you might find that most of your demands were unrelated to your teaching objective!

You can even have a more complicated list, where you examine the *type* of demand you made (see Figure 15c). How many different types of demand did you make? Which type did you concentrate on most? Was this what you would expect, given your objective?

These checklists can be as simple or as complicated as you'd like. They can be centred solely on one aspect of teaching, e.g. demands or feedback or prompts. At first it is certainly worth looking at all the different aspects in turn.

Alternatively, you can use a more complicated checklist which covers many different aspects.

In Appendix 1 (page 158), we have described such a checklist. However, checklists are designed to help you; so choose the checklist which suits you best.

3. Identify mistakes
Having worked through the recording with the help of a checklist, you may decide that some of your actions were mistakes, e.g. you gave very few models; reinforced inappropriate behaviour. It is a good idea actually to write down the actions you intend to take to rectify these mistakes.

4. Repeat the teaching session
As soon as possible, repeat the session with the child, bearing in mind the corrections you noted. This will test whether your corrections were effective in improving the session.

5. Analyse the repeat session
Finally, go through the repeat session in the same way as before. This will let you see if you did put into practice the action you had intended to take. More importantly, it will let you see how big a difference there is between the original and the repeat sessions.

Time well spent. This examination of yourself can take quite a lot of time. Indeed you may think the time would be better spent teaching the child. But that would be the case only if your teaching had no shortcomings. Often we are unaware of our mistakes, yet until we eliminate them, we must remain ineffective teachers. Thus the time spent on self-examination is likely to be well spent. Even examining a short session—say of five minutes—can be very informative: another reason for having short teaching sessions (see page 78).

However, we are not suggesting that you should record and evaluate every teaching session. Doing it when first embarking upon a new objective is probably all that is needed, for you will learn from your mistakes.

Also, as you become more experienced you will grow more aware of the effect you are having on the child during the

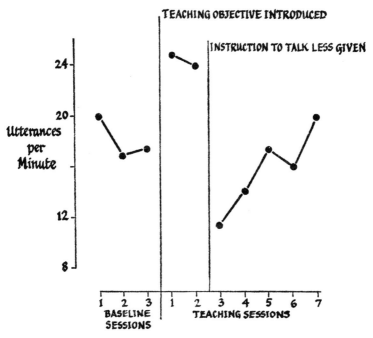

Figure 16

teaching session, and you will not need to carry out such a thorough self-examination.

We shall end on a note of caution, however. It is our experience that we teachers can easily slip back into our old ways. For example, we monitored one teacher's utterances per minute during the teaching sessions (see Figure 16). Once the objective was introduced the teacher began to talk a lot more than normal, which, as we discuss in Appendix 2 (page 163), is probably not conducive to learning. When this was pointed out to the teacher she immediately cut down her own talking. But note how it gradually increased again!

It is worth while giving yourself an occasional checking to see that you keep in trim!

Guided examination

As this is particularly useful for inexperienced teachers, this part of the chapter is written with them in mind. Here we shall refer to the 'experienced' teacher as tutor, for often her role will extend beyond 'examining' to that of tutoring the inexperienced teacher. A good example of this process is in the teacher-parent relationship (see Chapter 10).

The tutor's role is very important. An over-critical attitude will quickly discourage the teacher and lead to a loss of confidence. And when it comes to working with parents of handicapped children we need to be especially careful. If we are very critical of their behaviour, we can easily reinforce the feeling that they were responsible for their child's handicap. This can be a very real anxiety in some parents, although attitudes vary greatly. Of course, some parents anyway will be much better disposed to accepting criticism than others.

However, the tutor's aim is to help the teacher to become more effective and therefore *self-critical*. It is important to convey this from the outset. Here are some of the ways we have found helpful in doing this:

1. Research attitude
From the very beginning, the tutor has to make clear to the

teacher that there are no methods which will *invariably* help children to learn. All we can do is to try some methods which we think will work, on the basis either of our own past experience, or that of other people. All teaching is a case of finding out.

2. Demonstrate

The tutor should give the teacher a clear model of how the game or activity should be played, or how a particular technique is used (see page 94). Often this precludes many 'mistakes' (but see later). It also has the added advantage that you stress the positive rather than the negative.

3. Be self-critical

The tutor should be self-critical, in that if he or she was conscious of making any mistakes when demonstrating with the child, the tutor should point these out to the teacher. It is even better to do this when playing back a recording, and the teacher should be encouraged to join in with any other comments.

4. Reinforce good points

When reviewing the teacher's work with the child, it is vitally important for tutors to reinforce good points as well as noting mistakes. No matter how unsuccessful the session was, the tutor should try to find something good to comment on.

5. Make specific criticisms

It is demoralising for a teacher to be told, for example, 'that her attitude is all wrong' or 'that she is over-protective'. These general criticisms serve no useful purpose, largely because they do not tell the teacher how she should change her behaviour. Any criticisms the tutor makes should be very specific and are best related to a particular context, e.g. a teaching game or play activity. The teacher should know exactly how she should change her behaviour. Tutors should find the checklists described earlier particularly useful here.

We feel that all of these points will help to contribute to a good relationship between tutor and teacher. However, the basis of this relationship must be mutual respect and a realisation that each has talents which the other may lack. (See Chapter 10.)

Getting the message across. Finally, it is important that the tutor makes sure that the teacher has understood in what ways she might be hindering the child's learning, and how she should correct it. The following advice for tutors derives from our own experience.

Describe the mistake clearly and precisely. When you feel that the teacher is hindering the child's learning, you must very clearly point out to her how she is doing this. At first this can be very embarrassing, especially in the face-to-face situation. You may then be tempted to water down the criticism by hedging it around with qualifications, with the result that the teacher is left unsure as to what exactly it is that you want her to do. As one teacher told us, 'You were very kind, saying "well, you could have cut down", instead of saying "Shut up". Then I started to think: do they want me to shut up or don't they?'

Check that the required change was made. Do not take it for granted that because you pointed out the necessary changes that the teacher will go away and implement them. The teacher may find this very difficult to do. You therefore need to check, preferably by watching the teacher repeat the session with the child.

For example, with one teacher we recommended that she play a posting game in which the child had to say the names of objects before he was allowed to post them. We first demonstrated the game with the child, emphasising the importance of giving clear models of the objects' names. Unfortunately, we were not able to observe the teacher play the game, but we asked her to record a session at home. Figure 17a shows the percentage of models in the teacher's language was very much

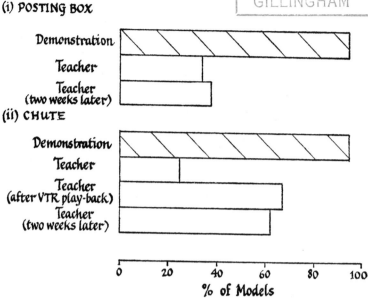

Figure 17a

lower than had been recommended, and two weeks later, the teacher reported that the child would not play the game. (See Figure 17b.)

We then introduced a variation of the game: putting objects down a chute. Once again we demonstrated this, then we observed and recorded on video-tape the teacher playing the game. Again she used very few models. After this session we replayed the video-tape and pointed out to her what she should *not* have done, described what she should have done instead, and reinforced any instances of 'desirable' behaviour. She was then asked to repeat the session and this time there was a marked increase in her use of models (see Figure 17a), and indeed in the child's target behaviour (see Figure 17b). This change was maintained when we next saw the teacher, two weeks later.

Not only is it important to check that the change is made, but periodic checks are also required to ensure that the change is maintained. As we noted earlier, it is all too easy for teachers to slip back into their old ways (see page 150).

The checklists described earlier can be used by tutors to record the teacher's behaviour, and to monitor changes.

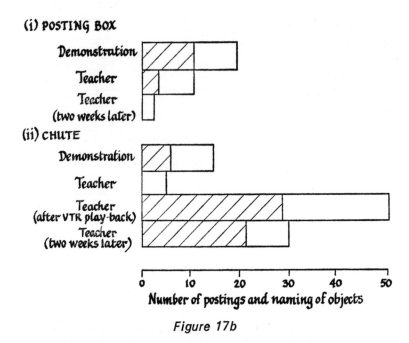

(i) POSTING BOX

Demonstration

Teacher

Teacher (two weeks later)

(ii) CHUTE

Demonstration

Teacher

Teacher (after VTR play-back)

Teacher (two weeks later)

0   10   20   30   40   50
Number of postings and naming of objects

Figure 17b

Experienced teachers. We would not like to give the impression that a guided examination is useful only with inexperienced teachers. On the contrary, it can be of great value for experienced teachers to share with one another their ideas of how best to help a child's learning. Indeed, in a sense we always remain 'inexperienced', for there is so much to learn. Within a school, teachers should explore the possibility of working together and making their 'self-examinations' into 'guided examinations'.

Finally, if you would like to pursue this topic further, Appendix 1 describes a fairly comprehensive checklist which can be used to examine teachers' behaviour.

Appendix 2 examines the teachers' role in language-learning activities.

Concluding comment

It has been said that special children need special teachers. When you consider some of the meanings of the word *special*, you realise that this is much easier said than done. But that should be our aim, and a step towards it is examining ourselves.

Special (adj.): *distinctive, not ordinary, intensively studied, unusually good*

Appendices

Appendix 1 :
A Checklist for Assessing
Teacher's behaviour

In this appendix we shall describe a comprehensive checklist which teachers can use to make a self-examination, or which tutors can use in a guided examination (see page 146).

Figure 18 shows the form we use. The actual items which are written on to the form can be varied. The following are examples of the type of items which can be included. All of these derive from the favourable and unfavourable learning conditions which we described in Chapters 6 and 9 respectively.

A. Teacher-initiated behaviours

1. Teacher models target behaviour

2. Teacher prompts child

    (*a*) physical;
    (*b*) gestural;
    (*c*) verbal.

3. Teacher makes task-related demand

    (*a*) child complies and is reinforced;
    (*b*) child complies but is not reinforced;
    (*c*) child does not comply.

4. Teacher makes the following different demands

These will vary according to the task. For an example see Figure 15, page 147.

5. Teacher makes demands unrelated to the objective

B. Child-initiated behaviours

6. Child's action is appropriate to objective
  (*a*) teacher reinforces;
  (*b*) teacher ignores.

7. Child's action is inappropriate
  (*a*) teacher attends to it;
  (*b*) teacher ignores.

Although it is possible to include all of these items on the same checklist, it is probably best to *select* those which you feel are particularly relevant to the situation in hand.

We also record the following information on the checklist (see Figure 18).

1. Length of session
You need to know this if you want to calculate the percentage of time the child spent 'on-the-task', or any frequency of behaviours during the session, e.g. number of models per minute. You can either time the actual teaching session or obtain it from the recording.

2. Teaching objective and materials used
It is worth noting this, especially when working from an audio-recording or when you might need to refer back to the checklist after a period of time.

3. Items
We write in the items which we feel are going to be particularly relevant.

4. Frequency
In this column we place a tick against an item every time it occurs. However, if the child is only repeating the same action,

F

TEACHER: *A.C.*   CHILD: *Matthew*   DATE: *31st March*   LENGTH OF SESSION[1]: *8 minutes*
TEACHING OBJECTIVE[2]: *Asking for the pieces from the picture form-board*
MATERIAL USED: *Home-made picture form-board and 'Give-Me game'* (Let Me Speak, page 121)

Items[3]	Frequency[4]	Comments[5]	Action[6]	Re-teach frequency[7]
Child makes appropriate action				
T reinforced	11	(1) Teacher demands perfect utterance before giving Matthew the piece	(1) Keep the child's interest by accepting his earlier attempts, then gradually encourage him to say the names more distinctly	1111 1111 111
T ignored	1111 1111			1111
Child actions inappropriate				
T reinforced	1111 1111 1111	(2) Teacher coaxes him when he wanders away from the table. Becomes a 'defiance' game	(2) Ignore him if he wanders off	1
T ignored				1111 1
Time child spent 'on-task': *3 minutes*	Percentage of total: *38%*		Re-teach: *7 minutes*	*85%*

Figure 18. Checklist for Observing Teacher's Behaviour

e.g. running around the room, then only place a tick when it first occurs. You might then want to note the length of time the action lasted, alongside the tick.

The main problem here is the criterion you set for each item. For example, what is counted as a 'model' or when will the child be credited with 'complying'? The more precise your teaching objective is, the easier it is to answer these questions of criteria. However, you must be clear in your own mind as regards criteria, and you must stick to them.

The chief advantage of keeping a frequency count is that it gives you a sensitive measure of the teacher's behaviour, which enables you to detect any changes that might occur.

5. Comments
Here we add any relevant comments about the quality or nature of the teacher's behaviour. This is particularly intended for use by tutors (see page 150).

6. Action to be taken
Here we note any action which should be taken to improve the teaching session.

7. Re-teach frequency
Here we note the frequency of items during the re-teach session, that is, after the examination (see page 152). A comparison of the two frequency columns will then show any changes which have occurred.

8. Time spent 'on-the-task'
You can really only calculate this accurately from a video-tape recording, in which case the total time spent on the task is divided by the session length and multiplied by 100 to give a percentage.

However, for record purposes you can make a fairly good estimate of the proportion of the time the child spent on the task using a five-point scale:

(*a*) nearly all the time;
(*b*) most of the time;
(*c*) half-and-half;
(*d*) some of the time;
(*e*) little or none of the time.

Appendix 2 :
The Teacher's role in
Language Learning

In this appendix, we want to concentrate on the role of the teacher in helping the child's language development. This is because many of the teaching activities with mentally handicapped children will be centred on language, as this is an area in which these children are often particularly retarded.

The teacher's role is particularly crucial in language-learning situations. Of course, all the points we made in the previous chapter apply to these situations as well, but some of those points have a special significance when it comes to helping a child to learn language. We first have to realise that it is extremely difficult to *teach* children language. The reason for this is that often our chief teaching method is language: we tell children what we expect them to do (see the tale of the demanding teacher, page 141). But it is impossible to use language to teach language. To try to do so would be equivalent to giving a non-reader a book called 'Teach Yourself to Read'! Yet we are so used to teaching through language that it is very hard to stop ourselves, with the result that we could make it even harder for the child to learn language. Here are some examples of ways in which teacher may hinder the child's learning:

Talking too much. When a teacher starts working towards a language objective, often the first thing that happens is that she talks a lot more than usual (see Figure 16, page 149, for an example). It is as though she is trying to do the learning for the child. But the danger is that the child will find it all the harder to work out what he is expected to learn. And if the teacher is doing all the talking, the child will not be able to get a word in!

Not responding to the child's language. In part this arises because the teacher is talking too much and does not leave any silences for the child to fill. But the other reason is that the adult is very used to being in the role of 'initiator' and having the child in the role of 'respondent'. Yet language is first and foremost a means of communication and that implies a two-way process. Therefore the child has to learn to initiate a 'conversation' as well as respond. He will only learn to do this through the teacher responding to the child's use of language. Often this will encourage him to use his language skills all the more.

Using language for different purposes. We use language for many different purposes, but the two main uses of language in teaching situations are:

(1) Using language to *convey information*—e.g. 'the cup goes on the saucer', 'this is a ball', 'John is eating'.
(2) Using language to *control* the other person, e.g. 'Sit down', 'What is this called?' Our language is aimed at getting the child to 'perform' a particular act, in this case the act of sitting, or that of naming an object.

When it comes to helping a child to learn language skills, such as the meaning of words, the first use of language is all-important. This is the model of language which we want the child to follow. This makes clear the meaning of words and shows how words go together to form sentences. Thus in a language-learning situation, the teacher's language should be predominantly of the first type (hereafter referred to as models) rather than of the control type. Yet often we confuse the child by having the balance the other way round, e.g. p. 153.

Our models of language are too complicated. To be useful, our models have to be matched to the child's ability to comprehend. Yet there are a number of ways in which our models can be too complicated and therefore unhelpful to the child.

Too many words. We use a dozen words where one would do. For example, we say 'This is a lovely red ball for you to play with' when teaching the one word—'ball'.

Complex sentences. Short sentences are much more likely to be understood. In the early stages of language learning, you can simplify them even more. For example, 'That's an apple that Fred's eating' can be simplified to 'Fred is eating the apple', and even to 'Fred eat apple'.

Using pronouns. We often use pronouns when talking about objects, e.g. 'Go and get *it*' or 'There *it* is'. A child may well wonder why we called the object 'ball' one minute, and 'it' the next.

Using the negative. Often we say 'that's not a ball' or 'Fred's not eating' if a child gives a wrong answer. Yet as we pointed out earlier (page 145), the child may not understand the meaning of the word 'not' and therefore he hears you confirm that the spoon he called 'ball' is indeed called ball!

Too many questions. We often use questions with the intention of getting children talking, but paradoxically they are a very good way of shutting children up. This is because

—many of the questions we ask children require only a Yes/No reply (e.g. 'Do you want the ball?), or a one-word answer (e.g. 'What's he doing?'). Such questions only encourage children to continue talking in single words.
—questions are always teacher-initiated (see earlier).
—we often already know the answer and if the child is wrong, he gets told off! With a 'true' question (i.e. you want to find out about something) this cannot happen.

These are just some of the ways in which adults make it more difficult for children to learn language. There are probably many other ways. We should be constantly trying to see our actions and language from the child's point of view. A step towards doing this is examining your own use of language. We shall now briefly outline a method for doing this.

TEACHER: *C.D.*   CHILD: *Tommy*   DATE: *31st March*   LENGTH OF SESSION: *6½ minutes*
TEACHING OBJECTIVE: *To use two-word utterances of the type '× + gone' and 'Give-me ×'*
MATERIAL USED: *Posting-Box with cup, ball, spoon, teddy*

Items	Frequency	Comments	Action	Re-teach Frequency
1. Number of utterances	1111 1111 1111 1111 1111 1111 1111 1111 1111 1111 1111 1111 1111 1111 1111 1111 1111 1111 1111 1111		Say less	1111 1111 1111 1111 1111 1111 1111 1111 1111 1111 1111 1111 1111 1111 11
2. Response to Child	1111 1111 1111	Very little child initiated language	Respond more to the child	1111 1111 1111 1111 1111 1111 1111 1111 1111 1111 1111
3. Type of Language				
(a) Model	1111 1111	Only used at the beginning	More models throughout	1111 1111 1111 1111 1111 1111 1111 1111
(b) Control	1111 1111 1111 1111 1111 1111 1111		Cut down	1111 1111
(c) Questions	1111 1111 1111 1111 1111 1111 1111 1111 1111 1111	Mostly requiring only one-word answer	Cut down	1111 1111 1111 1111 1111 1111 1111 1111 1111 1111
(d) Feedback 1111 1111				1111 1111 1111

Time child spent on task: *All the time*   Percentage of total: ....   Re-teach: *All the time*

Figure 19. Checklist for Observing Teacher's Language

Assessing teacher's language

The same procedures of self-examination or guided examination (see page 146) can be used here, with one major difference. You will probably find it more useful to use a different type of checklist, but, as before, this checklist is centred around the common mistakes noted earlier. However, we shall also describe a second method of assessing the teacher's language designed to be used with an audio-recording. This gives a very comprehensive analysis of teacher language.

Language checklist. Figure 19 gives an example of a language checklist. This is primarily designed to be used by an observer during the teaching session, although a teacher could of course use it in conjunction with a recording to make a self-evaluation.

The only difference from the earlier checklist (Figure 18) is in the items. A word of explanation about each:

(1) Number of utterances	A tick is placed for each utterance the teacher makes.
(2) Response to child	A tick is placed if the utterance was in response to the child's use of language.
(3) Type of Language	A tick is placed in the appropriate row.
(a) Model	Giving the child an example to follow or conveying information.
(b) Control	Using language to control the child's actions.
(c) Questions	Usually they start with 'what', although you can also ask a question by tone of voice—'you want to play with dolly?'.
(d) Feedback	Giving the child information as to whether he is right or wrong, e.g. 'Yes, good boy'.

N.B. Sometimes the same utterance can serve more than one function, in which case two or more rows are ticked, e.g. 'Very good, Joe, it is a red car'—Feedback and model.

F*

If you cannot decide which sort of utterance it is, then do not tick any.

With this checklist, a number of ticks have to be placed for the same utterance, e.g. if the teacher said 'It's a ball', then items 1, 2 (the child has said 'ball') and 3a would all be ticked. (See Appendix 1 for further information about this type of checklist, page 158.)

Simplifying the checklist. In order to get practice, it is better to start off with a simpler checklist, i.e. one with fewer items, e.g. use only items 1 and 2 or only item 3.

Analysing the checklist. The checklist can then be analysed in the following way:

Utterances per minute. How many utterances are there per minute? Count the number of utterances spoken and divide by the length of the session. Over 20 utterances per minute is rather a lot; there will not be much time for the child to talk.

Responding to the child. Divide the number of ticks beside item 2 by the number of ticks against item 1. The nearer the answer is to zero, the more the teacher was initiating and therefore not responding to the child.

Modelling language. How much of the teacher's language was a model for the child? To calculate this, divide the total against item 3a by the total number of ticks against items 3a to 3d. A proportion higher than 0·5 indicates that the teacher's language was mostly models.

These measures are also very useful ways of monitoring changes in the teacher's behaviour. For an example of this, see Figure 17a, page 153.

Language transcript. The chief disadvantage of the checklist is that you have no record of what the teacher actually said. At times, it is very important to have this, for example if you want to analyse the complexity of the teacher's language or the type of questions she asked. In these cases, you have to make a transcript of all that the teacher said, that is, write it out.

However, it is practically impossible for an observer to do this during the teaching sessions. Hence a recording must be used.

It can also be very time-consuming to make a transcript, so only use short sessions or parts of sessions.

Figure 20 shows the form we use when making a language transcript. The central column is used to write down what the teacher said. Each new utterance is placed on a new line. The left-hand columns correspond to the items of the language checklist (see above). As before, the column is ticked according to the utterance.

A note is also made of the child's language (or actions), particularly if related to the teaching objective.

Analysing the transcript. The transcript can be analysed in the following way:

Utterances per minute, Responding to the child and *Modelling language* can be calculated from the transcript in the same way as they were calculated from the checklist (see earlier).

Complexity of language. Is the teacher's language too complicated for the child? One way of detecting this is to calculate the mean number of words per utterance. As you are mainly interested in the models, count all the *words* in the utterances which have been classed as models. This will give you the number of words per 'model' utterance. You can compare this with the average length of the child's utterances, for instance if the child's average length is only one word and the teacher's is four to five words, there is a considerable discrepancy. It could indicate that the teacher's language models are too complicated. You can also note instances where the teacher has used pronouns, negatives etc. Put a circle round them on the transcript.

TEACHER: C.D.   CHILD: Mary   DATE: 20th June   LENGTH OF SESSION: 3 minutes
TEACHING OBJECTIVE: To name cup, car, ball, teddy in a posting-game
MATERIALS USED: (See above)

Teacher initiated	Response to child	Model	Control	Questions	Feedback	Teacher said	Child said (or did)
✓				✓		What's this I've got here?	
✓				✓		What is this called?	'Car'
	✓				✓	No, it's not a car	
✓		✓				You use it for drinking your tea	
✓				✓		What is it, what is it?	Goes away from the table
✓			✓			No, come here, I want you to tell me what this is first	
✓			✓			Tell me what this is and then you can go	
✓			✓			Say cup	'Cup'
✓				✓		Why didn't you say that when I asked you at first?	

Figure 20. Checklist and Transcription of Teacher's Language

Type of question asked. You can examine the questions which the teacher asked. It is useful to divide these into a number of categories, such as: Yes/No answer, One-word answer, Request for information (i.e. teacher genuinely did not know the answer). You can then calculate the percentage of questions which occurred in each category. This will let you see which type of question predominated.

Demand made on the child. You can also analyse the teacher's use of language to control the child. This related to our earlier discussion in Chapter 9, see page 142. You might ask questions such as, 'were the teacher's demands related to the task or were they irrelevant?' 'How many different demands did she make?' etc.

Relationship to child's behaviour. With this transcript you can see how the teacher's behaviour relates to the child's behaviour. For example, you can note what the teacher did before each instance of 'target behaviour' from the child (defined by your objective). You may then find that the target behaviour occurs much more frequently after a model than a question.

Concluding comment
We said at the beginning that you cannot *teach* a child language. But that is not to imply that you cannot help a child to acquire language. Indeed, the only way that a child will acquire language is with the help of someone who quite literally knows what he is talking about. Yet, to be useful, that help must be carefully matched to the child's present abilities. Assessing your own use of language will help you to achieve this match. (For further information about helping children's language development, see *Let Me Speak*.)

SECTION 4: WORKING TOGETHER

Introduction

Thus far we have concentrated on *the* teacher and may well have given the impression that he or she is all alone in helping the child's development. This is far from true. Every child has lots of potential teachers. At home, there are his parents, maybe brothers and sisters and grandparents, neighbours and friends. At school, as well as his class teacher, there will be other teachers, classroom assistants, dinner helpers and bus escorts. All of these people can be involved in helping the child to learn. And there are very good reasons why they should be involved. From the child's point of view, it will help him to generalise his learning to other situations, while from the other people's point of view, they will be given a purposeful way of interacting with the handicapped child and an opportunity to understand the child better. Thus, although one person may be solely respons-ible for selecting objectives and teaching methods, other people can be involved in teaching methods and the teaching.

The most important teachers
On the other hand, while a child can have many teachers, there can be little doubt as to who are the child's most important teachers. They are first, the parents, and second, the class teacher at school. The reason they are so important is that they spend far more time with the child than anyone else. Conse-quently, they will have a detailed and intimate knowledge of the child, and also many more opportunities for helping the child to learn, whether planned or unplanned.

They are important for another reason. Parents especially, but also class teachers, are responsible for the child. No one else has the same degree of responsibility. It is they who have to make all the important decisions. Indeed, in many ways, the parents' responsibility is far greater than the teacher's.

Yet although the parents and the class teacher are easily the child's most important teachers, the sad fact is that often each is working in ignorance of what the other is doing. The danger is that they may actually be working *against* one another. They may be emphasising different aspects of development, or using different methods, or they may have different criteria of success. All of which will only confuse the child. It is vital, especially with handicapped children, that parents and class teachers work together. Of course, we realise that home-school links can serve many purposes, but in this section we will concentrate on only one aspect, that is, the development of a 'teaching' partnership between home and school which is aimed at furthering the child's development.

Teachers and specialists
The theme of 'working together' extends beyond the home-school partnership.

Handicapped children often pose special problems for their teachers. The solution of these problems may require particular expertise, which the teacher may not have and could not easily obtain by herself. In these circumstances, the teachers should try to consult the appropriate specialist: physiotherapist, speech therapist, psychologist and so on. Note that we used the word *consult*. No specialist will have the time to take over the teaching. Instead, teachers have to learn from the specialists, so that the child can learn from them.

Now this idea of referring the teacher to a specialist is rather a novel one, for it is the normal custom still that only the child sees the specialist. As long as we continue to limit specialist contact in this way, we shall not be making the best use of our specialist help. In the final chapter, we shall be discussing ways in which teachers can work together with specialists.

Thus this section is divided into two chapters:

Chapter 10—describes ways whereby parents and class teachers can work together in helping the child's development. Methods for establishing and maintaining a 'teaching partnership' are described.

Chapter 11—describes the role of the different specialists working with the handicapped, and suggests ways in which teachers can work with them in furthering the child's development.

10 :   Home-School Links

Links between home and school serve many useful functions. But in this chapter, we want to concentrate on one particular aspect, that is the development of a 'teaching partnership' between parents and class teachers. This is especially necessary with handicapped children, not only because of their learning difficulties, but also because much of the content of the school's teaching is traditionally done in the home, e.g. language learning, self-help skills. We believe that the child is bound to benefit if the teaching which takes place in the home is co-ordinated with the school's teaching.

But the first question must be, 'who takes the initiative in setting up the partnership?' We have little doubt that it must be the school. In part, this is because of our educational tradition in this country, which tends to make the teacher the 'master' of the class and therefore of the child's education. Also, some parents may feel rather uneasy and shy with teachers. Perhaps their only previous contact with teachers was when they were at school. Given both these circumstances, it would be rather unrealistic to expect parents to take the initiative.

There is also another reason why the initiative should come from the school. When the child first starts school, the class teacher is very much the novice with that child. The parent is the 'teacher' with most experience. Therefore it is in the teacher's interest, as well as the child's, to get to know the parents and launch the partnership straight away. This will also remind parents that they have a continuing role to play, and that the school is not there to replace them, but rather to help them.

Given that it is largely the school who takes the initiative, the remainder of this part will be written with professional teachers in mind. However, this should not be taken to imply that parents have no part to play in establishing a 'teaching partnership'. On the contrary, we are assuming that they are willing and eager to take part. We suspect that with the majority of parents, this is a very reasonable assumption.

OPPORTUNITIES TO MEET PARENTS

Perhaps the first problem facing the teacher is to get to meet the parents. This can be especially difficult in Special Schools with their large catchment areas, and associated transport problems, or when both parents work full-time. However, with thought, such problems can be overcome.

Some schools organise a toy library for their parents, while others have a 'Mum's group' meeting once a week. Both of these are excellent ways for teachers and parents to meet fairly regularly in a relaxed and friendly way. They have the added advantage that parents can meet one another.

These sort of meetings can serve many purposes, but they do provide an excellent opportunity for a teaching partnership to develop between home and school. It is this aspect which we shall concentrate on in the remainder of this chapter.

WORKING TOGETHER

There are two aspects to developing a teaching partnership with parents. First, the teacher may need to help the parents become more systematic in their teaching. The parents, intentionally or unintentionally, are already teaching or have taught their child many things. But they could do this even more effectively if they adopted a more systematic approach. Hence the teacher will have to introduce the parents to many of the ideas we have described in Sections 1 to 3.

Second, the teacher and the parents will need to co-ordinate their teaching—not only in terms of objectives and criteria set, but also methods, techniques and so on. Here parents and teachers have much to learn from one another as they discuss and select alternatives. Most of all, they will learn about each other's aims and ambitions for the child. This can be particularly valuable for the teacher, for it is the parent who is, and will continue to be, ultimately responsible for the child.

We shall contrast two ways through which a teaching partnership can develop: (a) one-to-one contact, (b) parent groups. We shall first describe each method and then go on to outline the advantages and disadvantages of each. As the content is broadly similar with each method, suggestions regarding this will be given in a final section. We should point out, though, that we do not see these two approaches as alternatives. Ideally, both approaches could be used, each to a greater or less extent, according to circumstances.

Before moving on, we want to make two points. First, the methods for developing a teaching partnership which we shall describe derive from our own experience of working with parents of mentally handicapped children. We leave you to decide on their applicability to other situations and handicaps. However, although the methods might vary, the ideas underlying them can be applied to all situations.

Second, not all parents will have the ability or the interest to be full and active members of the partnership. It is impossible to state a percentage or to describe the characteristics of these parents. Our advice is to take nothing for granted; to give all parents the opportunity of taking part, and to start as early as possible, i.e. as soon as the child starts school, if not before (see page 191).

1. One-to-one

Here the teacher deals with the family on an individual basis. Note that we have used the word *family*, for with this method it should be possible for the teacher to get to know the whole family.

In order to get the partnership 'launched', you would need ideally a series of regular meetings with the parents. However, you can often achieve a lot in only one meeting, provided it is properly planned. These meetings can be at the parent's home or at the school, or you can alternate between these. Each place has its advantages and disadvantages.

Home-based. Going to the home will give you a chance to meet all the family, i.e. mother *and* father, brothers and sisters and grandparents. You will also see the child in new situations, for example helping in the kitchen, getting ready for bed, and you can observe how he interacts with his family. All of this will give you a much fuller picture of the child. You will also be able to talk to the parents free from the distractions and interruptions that invariably occur in school.

However, home visiting has some drawbacks. Often the visits are best done in the evening or at weekends, which is supposed to be the teacher's free time. Maybe we need to reconsider the teacher's job in Special Education, and make extra time available for home visits. But until such a change comes, home visits are, in a sense, voluntary work. Yet parents often realise this and to them it is an indication of your concern to help their child.

School-based. Seeing the parents in school and during school hours overcomes the main drawback of home visits. It also gives the parents an opportunity to see their child in a different situation. They can see him interacting with other adults and children, and may notice that he does things at school which he never does at home and vice versa. This is very valuable information for both teacher and parents.

However, it is essential that you make time to talk to the parents without the distraction of looking after the class. Hence you will need someone else to look after the class, and this often poses problems. School visits may also be difficult for the parents, either because of transport (could they come with their child in the school bus?), or younger siblings (would the nursery class-teacher or volunteer helpers look after them for a time?), or work (maybe they could arrange for an hour off, or else come at lunch time).

Whichever setting you choose, the advantage of the one-to-one approach over a group-based approach remains the same: that is, you and the parents focus exclusively on their child, you can demonstrate teaching techniques for the parents, and you can observe them teaching the child. Indeed, in the first instance, everything can be centred on specific activities with the child. However, you can then go on to draw out the principles (e.g. modelling, feedback etc.) which will apply across many different teaching situations with the child. The one-to-one approach enables you to work from the specific to the general.

The second advantage is that you can cater for the individual needs of the parents. For example, if they find it difficult to grasp a particular point, you can go back over it again.

However, the one-to-one approach has a number of disadvantages:

   (i) it is extremely time-consuming, especially if a teacher wants to involve the parents of all the children in her class;

  (ii) it can be difficult for the parents and teachers to find a place to meet which is free from other distractions;

 (iii) the parents do not get a chance to meet other parents. This can be a very valuable experience, for often parents do not otherwise have the opportunity to learn from each other's experiences;

 (iv) unless special efforts are made, usually only the mothers can participate fully. It is hard to involve fathers.

If, however, these disadvantages can be overcome, and they can with some effort and ingenuity, then this must be the preferred method. It is probably the ideal way of building up a working partnership, between parents and teachers. It is particularly suitable in the following circumstances:

  (*a*) when the teacher wants to gain experience of working with parents;

  (*b*) when the child starts school. This method is feasible if there is a staggered intake;

  (*c*) when the child is on the waiting list, but there is a link between the home and the school (discussed more fully later, page 191).

Before discussing the content of the meetings with parents, we shall describe the contrasting approach of group meetings.

2. Parent workshops

There are many forms which parent groups can take, but we are going to concentrate on one particular approach, called workshops. These were pioneered in this country by Dorothy Jeffree and Cliff Cunningham at the Hester Adrian Research Centre, University of Manchester, and have been used since by a number of schools throughout the country.

Briefly, the workshops usually consist of a series of weekly meetings (usually about ten in all), held on a weekday evening, each meeting lasting about two hours. No children are present at any of these meetings. The first half of the evening is given over to talks on specific topics related to teaching, for example assessment, observation, teaching techniques, language development and so on. After this, the workshop divides into small groups, each with a chairman, usually the child's teacher. These are the core of the workshop and it is from these that the name derives. The groups are *work* groups in that parents (a) can discuss the evening's lecture, and relate the content to their child; (b) can plan the activities which they will carry out with their child; and (c) can report on the activities they carried out during the past week.

The advantages and disadvantages of workshops are opposite to those of one-to-one meetings. Their great advantage is that a large number of parents can be catered for (up to 50–60 parents have taken part at a time); as the meetings are in the evening, both parents can often attend; there are no distractions, for all the participants have met for the same purpose; and finally, but perhaps most important, parents have an opportunity to learn from each other. Certainly this is what many parents appreciate most about a workshop. Rarely, if ever, will they have had the opportunity to talk so freely and intimately about their child to people who can really understand and who will share their problems and concerns.

The disadvantage of the group-based approach is that the

individual needs of the parents cannot easily be catered for. Also, compared to the one-to-one approach, much of the information has to be given first at a general level, and the parents then helped to relate it to their child.

Finally, the parents may have difficulty with transport or in getting baby-sitters, especially people capable of looking after a handicapped child. Your Social Services Department may be able to help here, or some of the voluntary organisations, such as Toy Libraries or local branches of the various Societies for Handicapped Children may organise a baby-sitting service.

With foresight, many of these difficulties can be overcome. Nevertheless, a workshop does require a great deal of careful planning and organisation if it is to be successful in developing a teaching partnership between home and school. Here are some particular points to note:

Speakers. These can either be teachers from the school or 'specialists', such as educational psychologists, advisers in special education, speech therapists, etc. It is most important that they be well briefed about the topics you (the teachers) want them to cover. They should be given a specific topic and told to avoid as far as possible any jargon or technical language. Ideally, all your 'specialist' speakers should be involved in the planning of the workshop from an early stage.

Also, the speakers should make full use of visual aids, particularly video-tapes. Parents tell us that they learn so much more from seeing a video-tape than from listening to a person talk. The time involved in obtaining the loan of video equipment, and/or in making tapes to show the parents, often proves well worthwhile.

Work groups. Probably the best way of organising groups is to base them around each class in school, with the class teacher as 'chairman' of the group. But if there are likely to be more than twelve parents in such a group, it is better to divide again into two groups if possible.

On the other hand, one disadvantage of basing the work groups around classes is that the children tend to be of similar abilities, whereas the parents could benefit from hearing of the experiences of parents with older or more advanced children. This need could be catered for by having a number of large group discussions involving all the parents. These tend to be more successful when held towards the end of the workshop, for by then the parents are used to talking in a group. You can also have informal coffee sessions when parents can chat.

Role of the teacher. One of the great benefits of the group approach is that the parents can learn from each other. Yet there is a danger that much of the talking will be directed at or come from the teacher. Her role should be much more that of a chairman, encouraging the parents to answer each others' questions and to exchange views. (This is not to say that she should never answer questions or give advice. Indeed, there will be occasions when it will be very desirable for her to do this.) But the role of chairman may well prove to be a new and possibly difficult one for the teacher. She may have to admit that she doesn't know the answers to some of the questions the parents raise. And even if she is confident that she does know, it is sometimes best *not* to give a direct answer. Parents are more likely to act upon information which they discover for themselves. Giving parents the answers precludes this from occurring. Sometimes, too, the question asked is not the real problem. A quick answer may mean that the parents never get a chance to discuss the topic which really concerns them. There is also the danger that the answer could be misleading, for the teacher may not have all the relevant information. In these cases it is probably better to direct the parents to the need for more information, rather than give an immediate answer.

In essence, the teacher's role has to be non-directive, except on those occasions when the group is in danger of getting side-tracked by a controversial but unrelated issue. In this case the teacher should suggest that they leave that discussion for another time and return to the topic in hand.

Monitoring meetings. After each workshop meeting, the teachers should meet to discuss progress and share ideas. In particular, they can note points which require clarification, or issues which the parents have raised in the groups which would not be covered in the original plan. It is worth while keeping a few evenings clear of talks, so that you can slot in 'extra' topics which arise during the early part of the workshop.

Timing of workshops. For continuity, all sessions should take place within the same term. The summer term is unsatisfactory because of family holidays, while the Christmas term is often an unsettled time within school. This leaves the spring term as probably the best, although it means travelling to and from the school on dark, wintry evenings. It also gives you the Christmas term for planning and the summer term for follow-up work.

For further information about workshops see:

> CUNNINGHAM, C. C. and JEFFREE, D. M. (1972) *Working with Parents: Developing a Workshop Course for Parents of Young Mentally Handicapped Children.*
> Published by National Society for Mentally Handicapped Children (N.W. Region) and Hester Adrian Research Centre.
> Available from N.S.M.H.C. (N.W. Office), Brentwood, Long Street, Middleton, Manchester.

Finally, we would like to emphasise that we do not envisage the workshops and the one-to-one approaches as being alternatives. Ideally, both approaches could be used together, with possibly one approach being used to a greater or less extent depending on circumstances.

Content. As the aim of parent workshops and individual meetings with the family is the same, that is, helping the parents to develop a more systematic approach to teaching, then the content of both will be similar. You will be introducing the parents to many of the ideas and techniques which we have described in Section 1 to 3. Note that we use the word *introduce*. Parents can really only learn about these techniques when they put them into practice, and this practice will extend beyond the workshop sessions or individual meetings with you.

There is one essential condition to success. You must be very familiar with, and experienced in using, these techniques yourself. You must also have confidence in your expertise, and be aware that you have something to share with the parents.

That being so, you will know best which ideas and techniques to concentrate on. We have probably already described the main ones in the previous sections, so in this section we shall suggest some approaches which we have found useful when presenting the techniques to parents.

Finding out. From the outset, make it clear that you do *not* know all the answers. It is no shame to say, 'I don't know', as long as you go on to add that *we* can try to find out. This attitude is not only honest, but it is a good example for parents, because it often enables them to work out the answers for themselves.

Using developmental charts. We and many others have found that Developmental Charts are a most useful way of getting parents started.

The charts give parents and teachers a common framework for talking about the children, in that they outline graphically the concept of child development. They also enable the parents to make a realistic, but at the same time hopeful, appraisal of their child's abilities, for they can see the progress their child has made as well as the developments which may lie ahead. The charts also introduce the parents to the idea of careful observation of the child's *abilities*, and they pinpoint specific skills which the parents may have overlooked (see page 28).

We introduce the charts in the following way. First, we offer an explanation of the content of the charts and how to use them; especially stressing that nothing should be taken for granted, and that every item should be tried with the child. Second, if working with an individual family, we work through one whole chart (usually Mobility) with the child present in the room. If we have not seen the child show a particular skill, we ask the parent to try and get the child to do it, for example, take his weight on his feet. In workshops, the parents read through the charts in their groups, and then discuss ways of trying out the items with their child, and the criteria they can use for successful performance. Third, the parents are asked to complete the charts with their child at home. At the next session with them, we compare their charts with ours and note and discuss any discrepancies.

Parents' concerns. Early on, discuss with parents their concerns about the child, particularly about their child's development, that is, things which they would like him to be able to do; and any particular problems that arise in handling him.

Hearing parents talk about their concerns will give you some idea of their priorities, and act as a pointer to the type of objective they might want to work towards (see page 47).

Observing the child. We continually emphasise the need to observe the child. Often the parents will be vague about their child's behaviour. Therefore, following on from the charts and discussion of concerns, we set the parents the task of observing particular behaviours and recording their frequency by means of a simple checklist. This introduces them to the idea of assessment through observation and the need to be specific (see page 31).

Selection of objective. We try to get parents to this stage as soon as possible. It is at this stage that the parents feel that they are really starting to help their child. Ideally the first objective should be one which can be obtained easily and quickly. If the parents experience success early on, they will be all the keener to learn more.

However, this can be a difficult step and often we need to give parents a great deal of help at this stage, maybe even suggesting an objective. This gives them a model which they can use for subsequent objectives, and emphasises the need to take small steps at a time.

Discussion of methods. We discuss with parents possible ways of achieving their objective, outlining a variety of methods (e.g. see *Let Me Speak*). Throughout, we encourage them to come up with ideas or to modify our ideas to suit themselves.

Groups in workshops can be especially useful here, as parents can share their ideas with one another, perhaps benefiting from someone's past experience. The parents should be encouraged to give reasons why they would use or not use a particular method. They should also be encouraged to try a method rather than dismiss it as not 'practical', which some may be inclined to do.

Demonstrate. Throughout we try to demonstrate the teaching games for the parents: how to use the toys, what we mean by 'prompts', 'modelling' etc. When working on a one-to-one basis you can do this with the child while his parents watch. For workshops, video-tape demonstrations are an excellent substitute. Alternatives to this are cine-films, or actual demonstrations with another adult taking the part of a child.

Did the message get across? You need to be sure that the parents have got your 'message'. When dealing with individual families, the easiest way to do this is to watch the parents with their child (we have discussed this at greater length in Chapter 9).

This is not possible in a workshop. Here the teacher might have to reinforce the evening's talk by asking the parents to describe, or even demonstrate, how they might use the techniques or games with their child. Getting the parents working actively in the groups is the best way of seeing that the message is getting across.

Specific tasks. Throughout the series of meetings, whether workshop or individually based, we always try to have the parents working on a specific task at home between the meetings. The tasks will vary as the meetings progress: first completing Developmental Charts, later perhaps noting the frequency with which the child is using two-word sentences in play sessions, and then teaching the child to thread beads.

We suggest that the parents set aside about ten minutes every day to work with their child. This is probably the most important part of parental involvement, for this is the time when the parents should be putting into practice all the things you and they have talked about. They will also be establishing a routine which can be maintained long after the regular meetings have finished. It also means that they will have something to talk about, or to show you (and the other parents), at the next meeting.

Keeping records. We ask the parents to keep an on-going record of the child's progress during the week. This might take the form of diary notes, or a checklist on which they note the frequency of certain behaviours (see page 125). We try to keep these fairly simple, but we do vary it according to the parents. These records form a basis for discussion about the child at the next meeting. They also help the parents become more observant and systematic in their teaching, and make it easier for them to see the child progressing.

Summary
Finally, here are the main points which we feel are most important in developing a successful teaching partnership with parents:

(1) *Careful planning.* Know in advance the ideas you want to get across to the parents.
(2) *Specific content.* Concentrate on a few specific points at a time.
(3) *Demonstrate.* Always try to demonstrate rather than only describe the games, techniques etc.

(4) *Check that the parents have understood.* Don't assume that because you have told or shown the parents what to do, they will then do it properly. You need to check.

(5) *Homework.* Agree with the parents on the *specific* activities that they should concentrate on at home.

(6) *Experience success.* It is important that the parents should experience success early on, for this will increase their confidence and enthusiasm. Therefore, start with objectives which are quickly and easily attained. Take small steps at a time.

(7) *Keep in touch.* The methods we have described are primarily ways of *launching* the partnership. Together, you will have to evolve ways of maintaining the contact.

The pre-school child

Lastly, we want briefly to examine possible links between school and home even before the child starts to attend school full-time.

This is a time when parents often get very little help, and yet it is then that they are most eager to do all that they can to help their child. The child too will benefit, for any gains made during this period will help him later.

But although there is a need, little is done at present to meet that need. In part this is because there is no one professional adequately equipped with time or experience to help parents in this way. However, things are changing and some authorities are developing new services for the pre-school child and his . family.

Links with special schools. Some authorities encourage parents to contact their local special school as soon as the child's handicap is recognised. The head teacher may hear about the child from the Health Visitor and may visit the family to establish contact. The school may have regular coffee mornings (e.g. monthly) for these parents, or else may invite the parents along to a 'Mum's group' or Toy Library meeting. This can be an efficient way of keeping in touch. It also gives the parents a

G

chance to meet others. These parents can also be invited to any workshop or evening meetings.

Peripatetic teacher. This is a teacher who is solely employed to visit parents in their own homes. She may start calling as soon as the child's handicap is recognised. Her role is to encourage and to help the parents play an active part in helping their child's development. As she can only be with each parent for a short time once a week, or once a fortnight, the parents remain the child's only 'teacher'. However, the peripatetic teacher can work with the parents on the one-to-one basis outlined earlier. She usually maintains close links with the local special school, and especially the teacher of the reception class.

With both these services and other similar ones, the underlying idea is the same, namely that education begins at birth and starts in the home. Waiting until the child starts school means wasting valuable time.

Conclusions

A teaching partnership between home and school can bring many benefits to the parents, to the class-teachers, and especially to the child. It does require extra effort, it will bring disappointment, maybe even disputes and disagreements. Yet the risk is small and we cannot help but feel that such a partnership may be one of the biggest single advances in the education of the handicapped.

11 : Working with Specialists

In this chapter we want briefly to describe the different specialists who are likely to be involved with handicapped children, and to outline the sort of help a teacher could expect to receive from them. We shall make some suggestions as to how teachers could set about enlisting the help of a specialist.

Of necessity, our comments about specialists must be rather general. There are no such people as typical doctors or psychologists. Although some may be specialists in their own particular discipline, they may have had little experience of handicapped children and may not be able, or even interested enough, to help. Others, however, may have taken a particular interest in handicapped children and will have a wealth of experience to share with you. Sometimes, too, this experience will extend across other disciplines, so that their professional label, such as 'physiotherapist', may not do justice to the full range of their expertise—although these people are still the exception rather than the rule. In all professions the amount of training for working with handicapped children is still a small proportion of the total. Specialists are trained to deal with a wide range of clients, sometimes of all ages, and with many different problems.

The following outline of what each specialist does is only intended as a rough guide. Our suggestions as to how to contact them are tentative, in that there may be different procedures around the country. We have deliberately omitted some specialists from the list, e.g. social workers, GP's etc., because we want to concentrate on specialists who could help the *teacher* (whether parent or a teacher in school) who wants to further the child's development.

Specialists

Paediatricians are doctors specialising in treating children. They are usually involved in the diagnosis of handicap, particularly of those handicaps present at birth. Paediatricians are based in the larger General Hospitals and of course in maternity and children's hospitals. Children with obvious handicaps at birth will automatically be referred to the paediatrician by the hospital. Otherwise, referral is through a GP.

The paediatrician's role is largely concerned with medical care. Where necessary he will prescribe drugs for the child and will be able to advise on the potential side-effects. He will also arrange for the child to be seen by other specialist doctors, as it is thought necessary, for example orthopaedic surgeons, eye specialists and so on, or will refer the child to appropriate therapists.

School doctors are not necessarily paediatricians. Their role is screening children for potential problems and arranging for a child to be seen by other specialists for further assessment. Teachers should approach their school doctor in the first instance in relation to any question that appears to be a medical one.

Health visitors are qualified nurses with additional training in community work. They are required by law to visit all homes with a new-born baby, and they retain a responsibility for the family until the child is five years old. They are involved in the initial screening for potential handicaps, such as deafness. They can advise on general 'care' problems such as feeding, diet, sleeping. However, with handicapped children they are starting to develop a wider role which includes a concern with the child's total development, and may therefore be able to advise on suitable play activities, for instance. Health Visitors can be contacted either through your GP or local Health Clinic.

Audiologists are trained in testing a child's hearing and in the diagnosis of any hearing difficulties. They can provide fairly accurate estimations of the nature and extent of any hearing loss, and where appropriate will recommend suitable hearing aids. They can also advise on the handling of a child so as to maximise whatever hearing the child has, or to compensate for the hearing loss. Referral can be through the school doctor or nurse, the GP or paediatrician.

Physiotherapists are trained to make an assessment of a child's motor abilities and to carry out the physical treatment needed to develop or maintain the maximum amount of movement. They will be able to advise on how best to handle a handicapped child, especially one with cerebral palsy: that is, on carrying, sitting positions, etc. They can advise on the type of exercises the child needs and will recommend aids and appliances where necessary, such as calipers, or special clothing. They are usually based in hospitals, but are increasingly employed by local authorities to work in special schools.

Occupational therapists are often mainly concerned with the provision of suitable equipment to help the family of a handicapped child, for example they will arrange for wheel-chairs, special banisters on the wall etc. They can also advise on a child's movement pattern, particularly of the arms and hands. They may recommend modifications to toys and equipment or suggest exercises which the teacher could use with the child. They can also advise on the therapeutic use of art, music, drama and so on. More occupational therapists are now working in Social Services Departments and can be contacted through Health Visitors or Social Workers. With occupational therapists working in hospitals, referral is usually through the paediatrician.

Speech therapists are trained to deal primarily with defects of voice and articulation, but recently they have become increasingly involved with general language delay. Most speech therapists are employed by the local authorities and they tend to work in schools. They are able to advise on the assessment and treatment of speech disorders, and should be of help with furthering children's language development.

Psychologists. The primary role of psychologists working for the local education authority is still in the assessment of handicapped children with a view to school placement. However, they are becoming increasingly involved in the education of these children and should be able to advise on the selection of objectives, teaching techniques and methods of education. They may also be able to help with the planning of parents' workshops. Parents can usually arrange to see an educational psychologist through the head teacher, or they can contact the School Psychological Service direct.

Psychologists also work in hospitals and children will be referred to them by paediatricians. In the past this has tended to be for assessment purposes only, but recently these psychologists too have become involved in the teaching of the handicapped child.

These are the main specialists likely to be involved with the education of the handicapped child; although there are others whom you could also consult, for example peripatetic teachers of the deaf, or blind.

Working with specialists

Many handicapped children have special problems which require specialist help. Sadly there are not, and probably never will be, enough specialists to cope with all the children needing help. If we are to make the best use of whatever specialist help we have, then we must use it carefully and efficiently. But first, we should make clear our idea of what the specialist's role should be with handicapped children, and in particular, the role of the speech therapist and physiotherapist. We envisage these therapists as *consultants* to teachers: helping with the assessment of the child and in the planning of treatment and teaching programmes, but rarely actually carrying these out.

These would continue to be the job of the teacher. Freeing our therapists from this aspect of their work would mean that their expertise would be available to help a greater number of children and their teachers.

However, we realise that this requires a change in the attitude of both teachers and therapists.

Teachers have to realise that just because the child is seen by a therapist for fifteen minutes or so, once a week, this is no excuse for them to be no longer concerned about that aspect of the child's development. On the contrary, if full use is to be made of that time with the specialist, the teacher must be fully aware of what the therapist is doing so that she can continue the work during the rest of the week. This applies both to home and school.

Similarly, therapists have to realise that their expertise lies not in the techniques they use, but in the diagnosis and planning of suitable remedial and developmental procedures. Therefore it is not a dilution of their profession if 'untrained' people are shown the techniques and encouraged to use them on their behalf and under their supervision.

However, we have to admit that some specialists do not agree with this view. This means that they may be reluctant to share their expertise with teachers. Other specialists, perhaps the more inexperienced, may lack the confidence to act as consultants. And of course, this happens with teachers too. People cannot be forced to work together, but the following points may help teachers and specialists to develop a working partnership.

Selective referrals. You will make better use of your specialist resources if you select only those children whom you feel would benefit from particular specialist help. Do not shirk this decision by referring all the children to every specialist. This only means that the specialist has less time to spend with the children who really do need help.

Face-to-face. Try to be present when the child sees the specialist, or at least arrange a time to discuss the child with the specialist.

Written reports are no substitute for the dialogue which the interview can offer; for here your questions can be answered immediately, your reservations expressed and joint plans made for future action.

Pinpoint specific questions. Know in advance the topics you want to discuss with the specialist. The more specific your questions, the more benefit the specialist can be to you.

Provide relevant information. Try to provide the specialist with all the *relevant* information you have, but present it briefly and succinctly. A summary of the child's abilities sent in advance of the meeting might be helpful. (A developmental chart can prove useful here, see page 23.) Also briefly outline the aspects of development which you have been concentrating on with the child.

Observe them working with the child. This is particularly valuable with physiotherapists and speech therapists, and is a definite must if you are going to use any of their techniques. You learn so much more from seeing techniques demonstrated than from hearing or reading about them. It is best to concentrate on one child per session, and in particular, on the one whom you will be working with most.

Try the techniques under their guidance. You should first try out the techniques with the child when the therapist is present, so that you will know straight away whether you are using them correctly. (A video-tape playback can be most useful here, see Chapter 9.)

Co-ordinate your teaching. It is important that you attempt to co-ordinate the specialist's recommendations with other aspects of your teaching. This is especially necessary if there is any possibility of conflict between different approaches.

Keep in touch. This may be easier said than done, but nevertheless it is important if the child's progress (and the teacher's) is to be kept under review by the specialist.

Finally, we want to make three further comments about inter-disciplinary contact which we feel would help the development of teacher-specialist partnerships.

Case conferences. Although common in hospitals and assessment centres, these are a relative novelty in the school situation. This is a pity, for they can serve several useful functions. They enable all the specialists to inform each other fully about the child, and give them the opportunity to discuss a common course of action and review progress. In a school setting a case conference would also mean that a class teacher could have the benefit of other teachers' experience. The main drawback of the case conferences is the amount of time they can take up and the difficulty in getting everyone together at the same time.

Joint training courses. We cannot help but feel that inter-disciplinary contact would be helped if at least some of our 'in-service' training for professionals were organised on a multi-professional basis instead of separate courses for teachers only, or speech therapists only.

Teacher as co-ordinator. As long as we continue to involve a number of different specialists in the education of handicapped children, it is urgent to make sure that the various roles are co-ordinated. The professional best suited to the role of co-ordinator is undoubtedly the class teacher. She is the professional who has most frequent and regular contact with a child, and the one with the overall responsibility to help the child's development. However, we do not envisage the teacher as being merely a referring agent or a passive recipient of advice from different specialists. Rather we would see her as being the integrator and executor of a 'total' approach. The teacher is also the professional best placed to involve the parents in the whole process, and to make sure that they are not overwhelmed and confused by the information given to them by different specialists.

This role of co-ordinator is a new and very demanding one for the teacher. It is one for which she will require training, yet we cannot help but feel that such training will be best acquired 'on the job' and not in college or university courses. It is a role which the teacher should start developing now, for until we do become more systematic in the help we give the handicapped child, our efforts will not be wholly effective and the child will remain that bit more handicapped.